SO YOU THINK YOU KNOW YOU KNOW ALL ABOUT FOOTBALL

D1333387

SO YOU THINK YOU KNOW ALL ABOUT FOOTBALL

Summersdale Publishers Ltd
46 West Street
Chichester
West Sussex
PO19 1RP
UK

www.summersdale.com

Printed and bound in the Czech Republic

ISBN: 978-1-84953-763-6

Substantial discounts on bulk quantities of Summersdale books are available to corporations, professional associations and other organisations. For details contact Nicky Douglas by telephone: +44 (0) 1243 756902, fax: +44 (0) 1243 786300 or email: nicky@summersdale.com.

SO YOU THINK YOU KNOW ALL ABOUT FOOTBALL

JONNO TURNER

summersdale

ACKNOWLEDGEMENTS

Thanks to my family, who keep me solid at the back;
the Summersdale team, for putting in the legwork
in the middle of the park; my mates, for their loyal
service and perfectly weighted supply from the
flanks; and my star striker, Sian.

CONTENTS

INTRODUCTION

I don't remember falling in love with football. But I do remember when I first laid eyes on it. It was Chesterfield v Gillingham on a Saturday afternoon in 1993 – and it was freezing cold and raining heavily. I remember my programme getting soaked through, and the cover star, a lumbering defender named Darren Carr, fading and falling to pieces. As I left the ground, toes and fingers turned to ice, I don't remember feeling particularly moved. But, in some way, I was. I simply must have been. Because I asked my dad if I could go back the following week. And the week after, and the one after that.

That's where this love story began. Not so much a slap around the face, but a flame that wouldn't die. And 20 years later, it still burns. It burns as I'm driving the length of the country for an away game. It burns when the rumour mill begins to click every pre-season.

As they say, it's a funny old game. And it's a funny old life as a football fan. Between the car, the water cooler, the pub and the pie shop, we never tire of analysing and arguing with our fellow fan. Let's face it – there's an armchair expert in all of us. And with the rise of social media, it just so happens that those armchairs are now next to thousands of others.

So you think you know all about football? Well, you'll find quizzes throughout the book, and a big one at the end to test your knowledge of the beautiful game. But let's kick off with a look back through the history books.

FIRSTS

> *Some people think that football is a matter of life and death. I assure you, it's much more serious than that.*

BILL SHANKLY

Two hundred players, vicious battles, and a severed head. Nope, it's not the title of Roy Keane's autobiography – that's supposedly how football began in Britain, back in the year 700.

Forget neatly-trimmed pitches and undersoil heating – this game was an altogether different affair. When a Saxon army began kicking around the head of a rival prince they'd just defeated in war, they inadvertently invented the beautiful game.

It caught on. Whole villages would play kick and rush through streets and squares, over hedges, fences and streams. It was spontaneous, it was violent, and it was no holds barred. Punching and kicking was allowed – in fact, injury and death weren't uncommon – and it stayed that way for six centuries, until these practices were banned by King Edward III in 1331.

Nearly 300 years later, in 1605, football became legal again in England – but it wasn't until the 1860s that the size and weight of the ball was finally standardised, and the first 90-minute game was played.

And since then, football hasn't looked back. Even today, the firsts keep on coming. Players are training harder, feeling stronger, playing faster. Sponsorship, memorabilia and business deals are growing bigger every day. And with the emergence of greater innovation, such as goal-line technology, the game is being analysed and dissected like never before.

It's a fast-paced and evolving sport – but the spirit is the same. And that's why we love it – because, for 90 minutes, nothing else matters. Because, ultimately, behind all of the glitter, the glamour and the razzmatazz, it's just 22 players and a ball.

It's magical, it's simple, it's beautiful. And, luckily, the severed heads are kept to a minimum.

On 20 October 2001, Aston Villa keeper Peter Schmeichel became the first goalie ever to notch a Premier League goal, in a 3–2 defeat to Everton – a feat that's only been repeated four times since in the top tier.

Undersoil heating was considered a luxury until 1958, when Everton became the first club to install it. It cost £7,000. Toasty! Their innovative move turned out to be perfect timing, as in 1962–63, Britain experienced its coldest winter since 1740, with average temperatures plummeting to –6°C and a thick blanket of snow causing a total of 261 match postponements.

DID YOU KNOW?

Carlo Ancelotti's Chelsea became the first Premier League side to smash over 100 goals in a season as they stormed to the title in 2009–10.

The first time an England match at Wembley was all-seater was 28 March 1990. But the numb bums were worth it – the Three Lions won 1–0.

The first ever Premier League goal was scored by Sheffield United hotshot Brian Deane on 15 August 1992 – a trademark header 5 minutes into the game against Manchester United at Bramall Lane. In 1996–97, Newcastle United's Alan Shearer became the first player to win the Golden Boot for two different clubs – having scooped it for Blackburn Rovers the season before. Since then, both Jimmy Floyd Hasselbaink and Robin Van Persie have matched the Geordie's achievement.

Dennis Clarke has a unique place in footballing history. He was the first ever substitute to be used in an FA Cup final, replacing John Kaye for West

Bromwich Albion as they ran out 1–0 winners against Everton in 1968.

Welsh wizard Robert Earnshaw is the first (and only) player to score a hat-trick in the Premier League, the Championship, League One, League Two, League Cup, FA Cup and for his country!

QUIDS IN

Trevor Francis is famous for being Britain's first ever £1 million player – but what about the first £2 million player? Well, that was Manchester United's Mark Hughes, who made the switch to Barcelona in 1986. He only managed four goals at the Nou Camp before returning to Old Trafford two years later.

Celtic's Billy McNeill became the first British captain to lift the European Cup in 1967.

Kevin Moran holds the dubious honour of being the first ever player to be red-carded in an FA Cup final. He got his marching orders playing for Manchester United against Everton in 1985.

In 1995, Everton's Gary Ablett became the first player to win the FA Cup with both Merseyside clubs, after lifting the same trophy with Liverpool in 1988–89.

Ian Porterfield became the first manager to be sacked in the Premier League era, when Chelsea gave him the nudge in February 1993. There have been over 170 managerial changes in the top tier since then.

The English FA was formed in 1863, when 12 clubs and schools gathered to make the sport of Association Football official. Until then, each different club had played with their own rules!

In 1892, Lincoln became the first club to add 'City' to their moniker.

The first time floodlights were used in the English league was in November 1955, when Carlisle United faced Darlington in an FA Cup second round replay.

JUMPERS FOR GOALPOSTS

The first time goal nets were introduced to British football was back in 1891.

Bobby Charlton first used the term 'Theatre of Dreams' to describe Manchester United's Old Trafford ground in an interview in 1976.

In 2001–02, Arsenal became the first ever Premier League team to score in every game they played that season – a whopping 38 outings without a duck!

The first match to be broadcast on the radio was a First Division encounter between Sheffield United and Arsenal in 1927.

In an attempt to keep the interest of players and supporters who would otherwise have nothing to play for at the end of a long season, the Football League first introduced a play-off system in 1986–87. In 1989, it was adapted to only include the four clubs who'd just missed out on automatic promotion.

Wolverhampton Wanderers and Tottenham Hotspur became the first two English clubs to face each other in a major European final in 1972. Spurs went on to win the UEFA Cup 3–2 on aggregate.

The first father and son to win caps for England were George Eastham Snr and Jnr in 1935 and 1963. While his dad appeared for the Three Lions just once,

George Jnr went on to secure 19 caps – and was part of the 1966 World Cup winning squad.

GAME OF TWO HALVES

Aston Villa's first ever game took place in 1874 against Aston Brook St Mary's rugby team. The first 45 minutes consisted of rugby, the second 45 minutes of football.

In 2006–07, Stockport County became the first Football League club in 119 years to go nine games without shipping a goal.

No English-born manager has ever won the Premier League. Who will be the first?

 Arsenal's Pat Rice became the first ever player to appear in five FA Cup finals for the same club – chalking up a quintet of appearances for the Gunners between 1971 and 1980.

White footballs were first introduced to English football in 1951.

The world's first football club was Sheffield FC, founded in October 1857.

In Wayne Rooney's first game for Manchester United, he smashed a hat-trick in a 6–2 thrashing of Turkish giants Fenerbahçe on 28 September 2004.

The rippling effect created when fans in stadiums briefly stand and cheer at just the right moment is popularly known as the 'Mexican Wave'. No one is certain when it first appeared, but it became world famous during the 1986 World Cup in – you guessed it – Mexico.

GOALS GOALS GOALS!

Stiff-collared Frenchman Eric Cantona was the first player to notch a hat-trick in the Premier League, when he plundered three goals against Tottenham Hotspur in a 5–0 victory in August 1992. But his goals didn't come for Manchester United – nope, it was his first club Leeds United who were the beneficiaries.

FIRSTS

The first ever player to score in a Champions League final, UEFA Cup final, FA Cup final and League Cup final was Liverpool's long-distance marksman Steven Gerrard.

Manchester United were the first side to score nine goals in a Premier League game when they thrashed Ipswich Town 9–0 in March 1995. Star striker Andy Cole had an unforgettable day – racking up five goals, and becoming the first top level striker to do so.

FIRSTS
QUIZ

----

1) Which player scored the first ever own goal in the World Cup finals?

2) **Italian defender Giuseppe Bergomi became the first footballer to do what?**

3) Why is Sheffield United striker Brian Deane's August 1992 goal against Manchester United so famous?

4) **Who was the first player to come on in an international game as a substitute for his own father?**

5) How did Israeli midfielder Yossi Benayoun strike his way into the record books whilst playing for Liverpool?

6) **When Cristiano Ronaldo notched a consolation header in the 4–1 defeat to**

Middlesbrough back in 2005–06, it was a goal that went down in history. Why?

7) Why was the winter of the 2004–05 season particularly eye-catching?

8) **What Champions League record does flamboyant Swede Zlatan Ibrahimović hold?**

9) Which two players were the first to score 30+ goals in the Premier League?

10) **Which great Dane became the first goalkeeper to score a goal in the Premier League?**

11) An 1891 first would change the face of football forever – what was it?

12) **For what dubious honour is ex-Chelsea manager Ian Porterfield known?**

13) What is Welsh striker Rob Earnshaw's rather unique claim to fame?

14) **What was unique about Wayne Rooney's first ever game for Manchester United?**

15) Stockport County hit the headlines in 2006–7 – but why?

MANAGERS

"

The problem with being a manager is it's like trying to build an aircraft while it is flying.

BRENDAN RODGERS

"

It's a poisoned chalice, football management. Living and breathing the game 24 hours a day, seven days a week, it takes over your whole life. There are joyous peaks and soul-destroying troughs. From the training ground to the boardroom to the changing rooms, being the gaffer can be a lonely job.

And when you're in the hot seat, you're only as good as your last game. Ex-Everton boss Joe Royle once said, 'I would never tell a plumber, a lawyer or a journalist how to do his job – but they all know better than me every Saturday.'

There are two jobs that everyone thinks they can do – Prime Minister, and football manager. But the truth is the armchair experts can be a fickle bunch. Get it wrong as a manager and you'll be castigated, jeered and booed off the pitch. But get it right, and you'll be awarded hero status – perhaps even your very own statue.

Here, we look at some who got it right, and some who got it wrong. You'll also find sprinkled throughout this chapter some pearls of wisdom from some of the most successful managers in the game, including Brian Clough and José Mourinho – gaffers who not only mastered the role, but also the art of playing the media.

The longest serving coach of all time was Auxerre's Guy Roux, who warmed the hot seat at the Stade de l'Abbé-Deschamps for a whopping 44 years between 1961 and 2005.

Manchester United's Alex Ferguson is widely regarded as the greatest manager of all time. The Scot scooped two Champions Leagues, three League Cups, five FA Cups, eight Charity Shields, ten Premier Leagues and a Cup Winner's Cup during his time at Old Trafford.

Some managers are so good that they can cross even the biggest divides. Take Brian Clough, for example. He led Derby County to the First Division title in 1971–72, before pitching up at their biggest rivals Nottingham Forest half a decade later, and inspiring the Reds to European glory twice on the trot. He's now a hero in both cities.

PEARLS OF WISDOM

BRIAN CLOUGH

Teams managed: Hartlepools United (1965–67), Derby County (1967–73), Brighton & Hove Albion (1973–74), Leeds United (1974), Nottingham Forest (1975–1993)

'I wouldn't say I was the best manager in the business, but I was in the top one.'

'In this business, you've got to be a dictator or you haven't got a chance.'

'He's not actually a very good player but he's got a lovely smile which brightens up Monday mornings.'

On re-signing Neil Webb.

'I had a walk along the River Trent today. As you know, it's my normal practice to walk on it.'

'My wife said to me, "God, your feet are cold." I said, "You can call me Brian in bed, dear."'

'The only person certain of boarding the coach for the Cup Final is Albert Kershaw, and he'll be driving it.'

'God gave you intelligence, skill, agility and the best passing ability in the game. What God didn't give you was six studs to wrap around someone else's knee.'

To Leeds United hard nut Johnny Giles.

In 2012, 21-year-old Vugar Huseynzade was appointed boss of Azerbaijan Premier League side FC Baku, purely because he was good at playing the video game *Football Manager*. 'I've always wanted to work in football and have been playing the game since 2002,' he said at the time. He lasted two years before parting ways with the club.

Thick-skinned Jimmy Davies has been confirmed by the Football Association as the longest-serving manager in the history of English football, having coached Liverpool County Premier League club Waterloo Dock AFC for a massive 50 years between 1963 and 2013.

SEEING RED

Having been knocked out of the FA Cup in 2003, Manchester United boss Alex Ferguson was so furious with his team's performance that he kicked a nearby boot in anger – only for the studded specimen to fly up and hit star player David Beckham in the eye. Needless to say, sparks flew – and within months, the midfielder was on his way to Real Madrid.

PEARLS OF WISDOM

ALEX FERGUSON

Teams managed: East Stirlingshire (1974), St Mirren (1974–78), Aberdeen (1978–86), Scotland (1985–86), Manchester United (1986–2013)

'I remember the first time I saw him. He was thirteen and just floated over the ground like a cocker spaniel chasing a piece of silver paper in the wind.'

On Ryan Giggs.

'My greatest challenge isn't what's happening at the moment, my greatest challenge was knocking Liverpool off their f*****g perch. And you can print that.'

'Sometimes you look in a field and you see a cow and you think it's a better cow than you've got in your field. Right? And it never really works out that way.'

On Wayne Rooney's transfer request.

'Do you think I'd enter into an agreement with that mob? Absolutely no chance. I wouldn't sell them a virus. That's a "no" by the way. There's no agreement whatsoever between the two clubs.'

On the Cristiano Ronaldo to Real Madrid rumours. Ronaldo later transferred to Real Madrid.

'I used to have a saying that when a player's at his peak, he feels like he could climb Mount Everest in his slippers. That's what he was like.'

On midfielder Paul Ince.

During a pre-season friendly between West Ham United and Oxford United in 1994, Hammers manager Harry Redknapp got so fed up with the shouts of an abusive fan that he pulled him out of the crowd and put him on as a substitute! The ringer put his money where his mouth was, though – even scoring a goal, only for it to be disallowed.

In 2014, Real Madrid's Carlo Ancelotti became the first manager to win the Champions League three times – having lifted the trophy twice with AC Milan.

Alf Ramsey will forever hold an important place in English footballing history, having guided the Three Lions to their only ever World Cup win in 1966. He is also credited with being one of the pioneers of the 4–4–2 formation, a tactical triumph which went on to become a staple of the British game.

TOP GUNNER

As of summer 2015, Arsenal's Arsène Wenger is the longest-serving manager in the Premier League, having joined the Gunners in 1996.

PEARLS OF WISDOM

ARSÈNE WENGER

Teams managed: Nancy-Lorraine (1984–87), AS Monaco (1987–94), Nagoya Grampus Eight (1995–96), Arsenal (1996–present)

'A football team is like a beautiful woman. When you don't tell her, she forgets she's beautiful.'

'What's really dreadful is the diet in Britain. The whole day you drink tea with milk and coffee with milk and cakes. If you had a fantasy world of what you shouldn't eat in sport, it's what you eat here.'

'I did not see the incident.'

On his curious inability to see fouls committed by his own players.

'At some clubs success is accidental. At Arsenal, it's compulsory.'

'Ferguson is out of order. He has lost all sense of reality. He's going out looking for confrontation, and then asking the person he is confronting to apologise. He's pushed the cork in a bit far this time.'

On his old enemy, Alex Ferguson.

'We don't buy superstars – we make them.'

THE SHORTEST MANAGERIAL REIGNS IN ENGLISH FOOTBALL HISTORY

Manager	Club	Duration
Leroy Rosenior	Torquay United	10 minutes, 2007
Dave Bassett	Crystal Palace	4 days, 1984
Kevin Cullis	Swansea City	7 days, 1996
Martin Ling	Cambridge United	9 days, 2009
Micky Adams	Swansea City	13 days, 1997
Paul Hart	QPR	28 days, 2009–10
Steve Coppell	Manchester City	33 days, 1996
Alex McLeish	Nottingham Forest	40 days, 2012–13
Les Reed	Charlton Athletic	41 days, 2006
Brian Clough	Leeds United	44 days, 1974
Henning Berg	Blackburn Rovers	57 days, 2012
Colin Todd	Derby County	98 days, 2001–02

DETENTION!

During his time at Hull City, boss Phil Brown was so embarrassed by his side's performance against Manchester City in 2008 that he insisted they remain on the pitch at half-time and delivered a headteacher-style dressing down to each and every one of them. It didn't work – they lost 5–1.

In 2013, Brighton and Hove Albion manager Gus Poyet was fired live on TV – the news leaking out while he was providing punditry on a Confederations Cup game between Nigeria and Spain.

Poor old Paul Jewell saw his Derby County side relegated from the Premier League in 2007–08 with a record no wins in the whole season.

In 1998, at the age of 61, Ron Noades became Chairman of Brentford – and immediately installed himself as manager, too. It was an inspired decision, as he led the Bees back to the third tier at the first time of asking, scooping the Manager of the Year award.

Not all great players find it easy to step into the hot seat. When Newcastle United hero Alan Shearer took the reins of his hometown club in 2009, he managed a win rate of just 13 per cent before being shoved out of the door at the end of the season.

In 2015, Grays Athletic manager Mark Bentley brought himself on as a sub with his side trailing 2–1. He scored a vital equaliser soon after, and then, when his keeper had to leave the field through injury, he put himself in goal – and saved a penalty. In an incredible turnaround, Grays won the game 3–2.

Alberto Suppici was the first boss to mastermind a World Cup final win – leading his Uruguay side to the debut Jules Rimet trophy in 1930.

UNLUCKY JIM

Jimmy Gabriel, who was caretaker manager of Everton for seven games in 1993–94, holds the dubious honour of being officially the least successful Premier League manager in history. The stand-in recorded six losses and one draw during his time in charge at Goodison Park.

THE TOP 10 MOST SUCCESSFUL MANAGERS OF ALL TIME

Manager	Silverware	Years Active
Alex Ferguson	49 major honours	1974–2013
Jock Stein	26 major honours	1960–85
Ottmar Hitzfeld	25 major honours	1983–2014
Giovanni Trapattoni	22 major honours	1974–2013
Walter Smith	22 major honours	1991–2011
José Mourinho	19 major honours	2000–present
Louis van Gaal	19 major honours	1991–present
Bob Paisley	18 major honours	1974–83
Ernst Happel	17 major honours	1962–92
Fabio Capello	16 major honours	1982–present

PEARLS OF WISDOM

JOSÉ MOURINHO

Teams managed: Benfica (2000), União de Leiria (2001–02), Porto (2002–04), Chelsea (2004–07), Inter Milan (2008–10), Real Madrid (2010–13) Chelsea (2013–present)

'Look, I'm a coach. I'm not Harry Potter. He is magical, but in reality there is no magic. Magic is fiction and football is real.'

After the goalless draw against Real Mallorca on his Real Madrid debut.

'I am no longer Chelsea coach and I do not have to defend them any more, so I think it is correct if I say Drogba is a diver.'

Jose re-signed Drogba in 2014 during his second Chelsea stint. Awkward!

'It is like having a blanket that is too small for the bed. You pull the blanket up to keep your chest warm and your feet stick out. I can't buy a bigger blanket because the supermarket is closed. But I'm content because the blanket is cashmere. It is no ordinary blanket.'

On a Chelsea injury crisis after the January transfer window closed.

'It is omelettes and eggs. No eggs – no omelettes! It depends on the quality of the eggs. In the supermarket you have class one, two or class three eggs and some are more expensive than others and some give you better omelettes. So when the class one eggs are in Waitrose and you cannot go there, you have a problem.'

On the lack of funds available to strengthen his Chelsea squad.

'Why drive Aston Martin all the time, when I have Ferrari and Porsche as well? That would just be stupid.'

On his squad rotation policy.

'If I wanted to have an easy job… I would have stayed at Porto – beautiful blue chair, the UEFA Champions League trophy, God, and after God, me.'

MANAGERS
QUIZ

----

1) Who is the only manager to have coached both the England and Finland national teams?

2) **Which young English manager received the Football League Manager of the Decade award in 2015 after leading his side to the Premier League for the first time in their history?**

3) Fiery midfielder Roy Keane once said, 'I didn't rate you as a player, I don't rate you as a manager and I don't rate you as a person.' Which of his coaches was he talking to?

4) **Arsenal boss Arsène Wenger is currently the longest-serving manager in the Premier League. When did he arrive in North London?**

5) Which manager became infamous for his 'I'd love it' rant during the pressured run-in of the Premier League season in 1995?

6) In 2004–5, which manager made the switch from fierce local rivals Portsmouth to Southampton, infuriating fans of both sides?

7) In 2014, a manager became the first coach to win the Champions League three times. Who was he?

8) 'I've never played for a draw in my life.' Which legendary manager said this?

9) 'Hasney's bust his hooter. He can smell around corners now.' Which manager said this of his injured Plymouth Argyle defender Hasney Aljofree?

10) Which European Cup-winning manager is a hero in two rival camps, Nottingham Forest and Derby County?

11) Ex-Norwich boss Nigel Worthington and ex-Wimbledon manager Egil Olson share which dubious honour?

12) Which world-class manager began life as an interpreter, working alongside Bobby Robson during his time at FC Barcelona?

13) How did Gillingham player-manager Andy Hessenthaler hit the headlines back in 2003–04?

14) Who was appointed as the English national team's first ever full-time manager in 1946?

15) In 2013, Inti Gas manager Rolando Chilavert was sent off – but why?

THE MEN IN BLACK

> *Referees should be wired up to a couple of electrodes and they should be allowed to make three mistakes before you run 50,000 volts through their genitals.*

JOHN GREGORY

Most fair-minded football fans would accept that referees today have something of a thankless task. Let's face it: we all make mistakes. But our gaffes aren't recorded, reversed, slowed down, analysed and pulled apart like the remnants of a chicken dinner.

Who'd want to be a referee? Nope, thought not. But it doesn't stop us from giving them grief. Far from it, in fact. Every Saturday afternoon between 3 p.m. and 5 p.m., you can guarantee that hearty choruses of 'You don't know what you're doing!' will ring around football grounds across the country.

If the modern game is a pantomime, then referees are both the evil stepmother and the Wicked Witch of the West rolled into one. But we should celebrate referees. After all, if it wasn't for them, the sport we love just wouldn't be the same. They're not just umpires; they're pioneers.

From the gentlemanly rulebook writers of the late 1800s, to Ken Aston's genius invention of yellow and red cards in the 1960s, and the introduction of goal-line technology within the last decade, referees have consistently been at the forefront of football's evolution into the game that we recognise today.

So next time you see a referee, smile and say 'Good morning'. Give him a pat on the back, buy him a pint. The referees of the world should be able to sleep soundly at night – safe in the knowledge that, hey, at least they're not linesmen.

At the time of the first FA Cup and international fixtures, two umpires, one per team, were employed as officials – and each side could appeal to them. The referee stood on the touchline and was only 'referred' to if the umpires couldn't agree.

Vanishing spray was used for the first time in the 2014 World Cup to measure out distances during set-pieces. It lasts for around 20 seconds before dissolving, and solved the age-old problem of defending players – who are supposed to stand 10 yards from the ball – encroaching before a kick is taken.

DID YOU KNOW?

Yellow and red cards were invented by English referee Ken Aston, and introduced at the 1970 World Cup.

Referees first used whistles in England in 1878. The first game ever credited with the use of a whistle was at Nottingham Forest. Before this day, refs used handkerchiefs to call for a stoppage in play.

Welsh official Clive Thomas, nicknamed 'The Book' because of his rigorous application of the laws of the game, broke Brazilian hearts by denying them a 2–1 win over Sweden in the 1978 World Cup. The South Americans thought they'd won through Zico's last-minute header, but Thomas blew the final whistle a fraction of a second before the ball crossed the line, and ruled that the goal didn't count.

A match in South Africa in 1999 saw ref Lebogang Petrus Mokgethi shoot a player dead following a pitch invasion from fans. During the game between Hartbeesfontein Wallabies and Try Agains, a Wallabies player left the field and returned with a knife. It later transpired that the trouble was due to betting on the match.

The decision in 1902 to award penalties for fouls committed in an area 18 yards from the goal line and 44 yards wide, led to the creation of both the penalty box and penalty spot.

As the sport grew in popularity in the late 1800s, there was an assumption that a gentleman would never deliberately commit a foul. As the game became more competitive, the penalty – or as it was originally called, 'The kick of death' – was introduced in 1891.

HANDBAGS AT DAWN

In a match against Aston Villa in 2005, Newcastle United were already down to ten men after a deliberate handball by Steven Taylor. After an altercation on the pitch, two more players were sent off. A terrible position for a team to be in, made even worse by the fact the two players sent off were Magpies midfielders, Kieron Dyer and Lee Bowyer, who had started fighting with each other.

Players got a shock during a five-a-side contest in London, when the ref, who had been on the receiving end of some player abuse all game, called the match off and left the pitch… only to return wielding an axe. Luckily, no one was injured, and the official jumped in his car and drove off. 'He went completely berserk,' said one of the players. 'He ran off the pitch and returned a few moments later stripped to the waist and waving a long axe around his head.'

WOULD YOU PEA-LIEVE IT?

It was so cold during an England Under-21s game with the Netherlands that the restart was delayed by several minutes because the pea in the referee's whistle had frozen!

During Nottingham Forest's 1984 clash with Anderlecht, there was something a little fishy about referee Emilio Guruceta Muro's performance. It was later revealed, ten years after he had died, that he had been paid the equivalent of €1 million to ensure that the Belgian side won the game – which they did, 3–0.

On 31 August 1996, Wendy Toms became the first female to referee a senior match in England – the Conference fixture between Woking and Telford United. After just 14 minutes Woking's Andy Ellis became the first player to be booked at that level by a female ref, for dissent. 'It's an honour,' he said!

The first ever player in the Football League to see red was David Wagstaffe, playing for Blackburn Rovers at Leyton Orient on 2 October 1976. Later that afternoon George Best, playing for Fulham at Southampton, was also red carded for swearing.

Alvaro Ortega was horrifically gunned down after officiating as a linesman during a Colombian match between Independiente Medellin and America de Cali in 1989. Organised crime was blamed for his death, as it was later revealed that Ortega had turned down a bribe.

DID YOU KNOW?

Goalkeepers were allowed to handle the ball outside of their area up until 1912, when the current rule, prohibiting them from picking up the ball outside of the 18-yard box, was introduced in order to create more goal chances.

Before a cup match in 2000, a club allegedly offered an anonymous official a bribe. However, this was no ordinary bribe – the club offered the referee the services of a number of prostitutes if he agreed to fix the match.

In the late 1930s, it was decided that the rules of the game needed a bit of a makeover. Englishman Stanley Rous was appointed to streamline the handbook – and he did such a good job that the laws weren't revised again until 1997.

FC Wijtshate were so bad in a 2002 match that the ref blew early to put them out of their misery. The man in black was Marc Gevaert, who ended the game on 85 minutes when Vladslo went 16–0 up!

'OI, REF!'

EIGHT FAMOUS GAFFES BY THE MEN IN THE MIDDLE

In the 2006 World Cup clash between Croatia and Australia, English ref Graham Poll showed Croatia's Josip Šimunić three yellow cards, before remembering to send the player off.

Diego Maradona got away with one of the most blatant and memorable rule infringements in football history in 1986, when he scored his famous 'Hand of God' goal, punching the ball beyond England keeper Peter Shilton in the World Cup quarter-finals to put his side 1–0 up. Tunisian ref Ali Bin Nasser argued he did not see the incident.

In 2014, Premier League referee Andre Marriner sent off Arsenal defender Kieran Gibbs for handball despite the full back being a completely innocent party. In fact, the crime was committed by his teammate, Alex Oxlade-Chamberlain, but despite the red-faced player's admission of guilt, the ref refused to back down, and Gibbs was sent trudging down the tunnel. Luckily, it didn't change the end result – the Gunners ran out 6–0 winners in Arsène Wenger's 1,000th game in charge.

Not everyone saw the funny side of Paul Gascoigne's humour. During a Rangers v Hibs match at Ibrox on 30 December 1995 he found the ref's yellow card on the pitch. He jokingly held it up to the ref before returning it to him. Ref Dougie Smith didn't see the funny side – snatching the card and booking Gascoigne for real.

In 2013, Bayer Leverkusen's Stefan Kiessling scored a header that never actually went in. Replays showed that the ball squeezed through a hole in the side netting – but the referee Dr Felix Brych awarded it anyway, despite mass protestations from unlucky side Hoffenheim. The game ended 2–1 to Leverkusen.

When El Salvador appeared at the 1970 World Cup finals, it should have been a cause for celebration – but instead, the headlines went to referee Ali Hussein Kandil. He awarded a free kick to El Salvador in their match against Mexico, but amid confusion over whether it was a free kick or a throw-in, Mexico took the free kick and went on to score. The ref, a little overwhelmed by the occasion, simply decided to go with it and award the goal, to the fury of the El Salvadorians. They refused to kick off, constantly moving the ball from the centre circle before booting it into the stands.

When Sunday League ref Andy Wain lost his temper in the middle of a match, he followed the letter of the law and showed himself a straight red card. Officiating a game between Peterborough North End and Royal Mail AYL in 2005, he awarded a goal, to which the opposition goalkeeper protested – causing Wain to throw down his whistle and square up to the keeper. When the red mist faded, he promptly sent himself off and the match was abandoned.

English referee Stuart Atwell burst on to the scene in style when he became the youngest person to ever to ref in the Premier League at the age of 25 in 2008, but that's not what he's remembered for. On 20 September 2008, he awarded a goal to Reading in their game against Watford – although replays later showed that the ball had actually gone 4 yards wide of the net. The incident became known as the 'ghost goal', and poor old Atwell has never quite lived it down.

THE MEN IN BLACK
QUIZ

----

1) In what year were yellow and red cards first introduced?

2) **English referee Howard Webb is widely regarded as one of the best ever – but what was so special for him about 2010?**

3) When penalty kicks were awarded back in 1901, what were they known as?

4) **Who decides on how much injury-time should be played – the referee or the fourth official?**

5) What year did the first female referee take charge of an English senior match?

6) **Why did Dougie Smith book Rangers' Paul Gascoigne in a game against Hibernian in 1995?**

7) Which Argentinian legend shocked the world by scoring with his hand during the 1986 World Cup semi-final – and getting away with it?

8) **What changed for goalkeepers in 1912?**

9) Before whistles were introduced, what did referees use to halt play?

10) **Why did English ref Graham Poll hit the headlines at the 2006 World Cup?**

COULD YOU BE A REF? TRY THESE QUESTIONS AND SEE IF YOU MEASURE UP...

11) What's the minimum height of a corner flag?

12) **Team A's star striker scores his hat-trick goal in front of his home fans. He runs into the crowd to celebrate. Is this an offence, and if so, how should it be punished?**

13) Is a referee obliged to always stop the game if a player is injured while the ball is in play?

14) **You're the man in the middle, and a striker hits a shot so powerful that you can't get out of the way before it hits you on the hand. What's the call?**

15) As soon as the referee blows his whistle for a penalty kick to be taken, can the goalkeeper move off his line?

16) **True or false – when a dropped ball is awarded, only one member of each team may contest for the ball.**

17) A player from Team B hits a shot so poor that it skews to the right and rebounds off the corner flag. What should the referee do?

18) **Team A's striker is running through on goal when a spectator blows a whistle and the player stops, thinking it's a signal from the referee. How does play restart?**

19) A goalkeeper can only handle the ball inside his own penalty area. Can a goalkeeper leave the penalty area and take a throw-in?

20) **Team A is awarded a free kick in their own half. A defender goes to kick the ball, but realises that his kick isn't very powerful, and instead turns around and passes back to his goalkeeper. However, the goalie isn't looking and the ball rolls into the net. What's the call?**

THE WORLD CUP

> *The World Cup is a very important way to measure the good players, and the great ones. It is a test of a great player.*
>
> PELÉ

Ah, the World Cup. A competition where heroes are born and legends are made. The biggest trophy in all of football – and many would say the pinnacle of team sports. There's something about the clash of cultures, the sights and the sounds, the special moments and the memories that makes this competition stand out from the rest.

Ever since it began back in 1930, the World Cup has consistently given us the best that this game has to offer. Twists, turns, and plenty of thrills.

Ferenc Puskás, Pelé, Bobby Moore. Johan Cruyff, Diego Maradona, Ronaldo. They've all made their mark on the biggest stage of all – the ultimate test for any player.

And it breeds passion, excitement and enthusiasm. For one month every four years, even the most cynical and jaded fan can't resist getting out the flags, slapping on the face paint and letting out a hearty roar at the TV. Work stops, friends meet up and families gather round. Whole nations stand still and the world watches.

Well, they don't call it the greatest show on earth for nothing.

Robert Prosinečki is the only player to have scored World Cup goals for two different national teams – Yugoslavia in 1990 and Croatia in 1998.

Russian forward Oleg Salenko scored the most goals in a single World Cup match, bagging five against Cameroon in 1994.

In 2014, Germany's Miroslav Klose scored his 14th World Cup goal – overtaking the Brazilian Ronaldo to become the top scorer in World Cup finals history.

UNLUCKY NUMBER?

Australia's Archie Thompson notched a whopping 13 goals in one World Cup qualifying game, a 31–0 win against American Samoa, in April 2001. That's more than double the amount of goals he scored at club level in the entire season!

The fastest goal in a World Cup finals game belongs to Turkey striker and one-time Blackburn Rover Hakan Şükür, who took just 11 seconds to hit the net against South Korea in 2002.

On their way to lifting the famous trophy in 2014, Germany appeared in the World Cup final for an eighth time – the most of any nation in history.

USA keeper Tim Howard had a busy night on 1 July 2014 – he made a record 16 saves as his side was relentlessly bombarded in a 2–1 loss to Belgium.

The first ever World Cup was held in Uruguay in 1930 – and was won by the hosts.

DID YOU KNOW?

As Brazil crashed out of the 2014 World Cup in a 7–1 defeat by Germany, they also made it into the record books, with the highest margin of defeat suffered by a host nation in the tournament's history.

The original World Cup trophy was named after Jules Rimet, FIFA President from 1921–54.

No country has won the Eurovision Song Contest and the World Cup in the same year. In 1982, West Germany came close by winning the song contest – but the soccer team went on to lose the World Cup final against Italy.

IT'S MILLA TIME

In 1994, Cameroon's golden oldie Roger Milla became the oldest player to score in a World Cup finals – he was 42 years young.

 The trophy has been stolen twice. The first was just before the 1966 World Cup, where it was found in a garden by a dog named Pickles. It happened again in 1983. That time, it was never found – and is believed to have been melted down by the thieves.

Due to World War Two, there were no World Cups held between 1938 and 1950. As a result, Italy were champions for a record 16 years, after scooping back-to-back trophies in 1934 and 1938.

Who says there's no such thing as a home advantage? Out of the 20 World Cups played so far, six have been won by the host country.

Brazil is the only country to have appeared in every World Cup tournament – from 1930 to 2014.

Serbian gaffer Bora Milutinović coached in every tournament between 1986 and 2002, but for different teams: Mexico, Costa Rica, USA, Nigeria and China.

PUT IT AWAY, SON!

Swapping shirts was prohibited at the start of the 1986 World Cup as FIFA didn't want players to bare their chests on the pitch.

Colombia was originally chosen to host the 1986 World Cup, but FIFA later awarded the tournament to Mexico after the South American nation backed out.

No host country had ever been knocked out in the First Round until South Africa were sent packing in 2010.

The first ever penalty in World Cup history was taken on 19 July 1930, by Chile's Carlos Vidal. It went on to become the first ever penalty save in World Cup history, with France's Alexis Thépot keeping the subsequent shot out.

'WHO ARE YA? NO... REALLY, WHO ARE YA?'

Numbers weren't used on players' shirts in a World Cup game until 1938.

The first live TV coverage of a World Cup took place in 1958 – it has since become the most widely viewed sporting event on the planet.

In 1974, Zaire (now the Democratic Republic of Congo) became the first African nation to play at a World Cup finals.

The first time that goal-line technology was used in a World Cup finals was Brazil in 2014. The first goal to be awarded because of it was an own goal – by Honduran keeper Noel Valladares against France!

Zinedine Zidane is widely considered one of modern world football's greatest players. But despite the accolades, Zidane is statistically the dirtiest player in World Cup history – receiving four yellow and two red cards, one of which was for his now infamous headbutting of Marco Materazzi in the France v Italy final in 2006.

The Netherlands is one of the best footballing nations never to have won a World Cup. The Oranje have made it to the final – and lost – three times (1974, 1978, 2010).

England's 1966 hero Geoff Hurst is the only player to score a hat-trick in a World Cup final, against West Germany at Wembley.

Hungary scored the most goals in any single World Cup finals game, thrashing El Salvador 10–1 in 1982!

Spare a thought for Scotland. They've made it to the World Cup finals eight times – and been knocked out in the First Round, well, eight times.

India reportedly withdrew from the 1950 World Cup when they found out that FIFA wouldn't allow them to play barefoot!

Italy's Giuseppe Meazza gave the opposition a laugh in 1934 when his shorts fell down as he strode up to take a penalty kick! Unfazed, he picked them up and still shot past the laughing and slightly confused

Brazilian goalie to send his country into the World Cup final!

 A peculiar twist to the 1958 World Cup finals was that all of the losing sides scored no goals.

Ferenc Puskás, widely regarded as one of the best players of all time, appeared at two different World Cups for two different sides – the first, in 1954 for Hungary, and the second in 1962 for Spain. He became a naturalised citizen of his adopted nation after emigrating there to play for Real Madrid during the Hungarian Revolution.

During the 1970 World Cup final, the Netherlands, famed for the introduction of 'Total Football', faced host nation West Germany. In just over a minute, the Dutch earned and scored a penalty, with the West German players having not even managed to touch the ball. West Germany went on to win 2–1.

THE WORLD CUP
QUIZ

----

1) When and where did the first ever World Cup take place?

2) **Germany's Miroslav Klose made history in 2014. Why?**

3) England's Peter Shilton and France's Fabian Barthez share a World Cup record. What is it?

4) **How many players have scored hat-tricks from the penalty spot during a World Cup tournament?**

5) Only two people have won the World Cup as both player and coach – who are they?

6) **When England lifted their only World Cup trophy in 1966, who was the coach?**

7) Which nation has won more World Cup trophies than any other?

8) **Robert Prosinečki holds the honour of being the only player to have scored a World Cup goal for two different teams. Which teams?**

9) What was unique about the 1958 tournament in Sweden?

10) **How fast was the quickest recorded goal in World Cup history?**

11) Which manager has won more World Cup encounters than any other?

12) **What World Cup record does England keeper David James hold?**

13) How many foreign coaches have won the World Cup?

14) **In the 2014 World Cup in Brazil, Mexico's Rafa Márquez made history. Why?**

15) Why does coach Bora Milutinović have a unique place in World Cup history?

THE EUROPEAN CHAMPIONSHIP

> *I still get goosebumps whenever I think about England at Euro 96. Managing there and representing my country provided the best moments of my life, which I will never forget.*

TERRY VENABLES

Since 1958, it's one of the biggest sporting events in the world, pitting national teams from every corner of Europe against each other, with thrilling results. But, surprisingly, the notion of a European international competition was not an easy idea to sell.

In fact, Frenchman Henri Delaunay, who pioneered the idea of a tournament, first pitched the concept to FIFA in 1927 – before even the first World Cup. And it took nearly three decades more for UEFA to be formed, and for them to decide to develop the original concept themselves.

Delaunay specified two things: first, that the competition should not harm the World Cup, of which he was a big fan, and secondly, that teams should not always meet the same opponents in the same group.

And so it began, the inaugural tournament taking place in 1960 in Henri's native France. The winners? The Soviet Union.

Unfortunately, Henri died in 1955 – too soon to see his idea come to fruition.

The 16th tournament, taking place in 2016, will see the competition return to France – arguably its spiritual home – for a third time. Hat-trick for Henri! As they say, good things come to those who wait.

The competition began in 1960 as the European Nations' Cup. Back then the final tournament consisted of four teams, each of which survived a knock-out competition played over the previous two years.

The 1960 competition was almost cancelled due to a lack of support after many countries left it late to apply.

The name 'UEFA European Championship' was adopted in 1968, the same year as knock-out preliminaries were replaced by the modern qualifying round.

The four-team final tournament was expanded to eight teams in 1980 and 16 in 1996, with 48 taking part in qualifiers.

Spain and Germany have lifted this trophy more than any other nation – achieving three wins each.

In the 2000 finals, England beat Germany 1–0 – their first victory against them in a competitive game since the 1966 World Cup final.

DID YOU KNOW?

The largest attendance in competition history was a qualifier between England and Scotland at Hampden Park for the 1968 competition, with a total of 130,711 people there.

In 1960 the Spanish team were withdrawn by their right-wing government rather than play the impressive, and Communist, Soviet Union.

The oldest player ever to appear in the tournament is Germany's Lothar Matthäus, who was 39 years and 91 days at the time of his last run out in 2000.

The trophy is named after Henri Delaunay, the central character in the development of European football and UEFA.

In 1964, the Netherlands were dumped out of the tournament by minnows Luxembourg. The tiny country of just half a million didn't win another European Championship qualifier until 1995.

In 1960, France goalie Georges Lamia shipped three goals in 4 minutes as Yugoslavia beat the hosts 5–4 in the semi-finals. The player went on to win just one more cap in his whole career.

The youngest player ever to appear in the European Championship final is Cristiano Ronaldo in 2004, who took to the field against Greece at the age of just 19 years and 150 days.

The 1992 European Championship in Sweden was the first major finals tournament where the players' shirts bore their names as well as their numbers.

In the 1968 tournament, Alan Mullery became the first England player to be sent off in an international.

'IT'S COMING HOME, IT'S COMING HOME...'

The year 1996, when the tournament was played in England, saw the release of 'Three Lions', by Baddiel and Skinner. The song went straight to number one – and was even a hit in other countries, climbing to number 16 in Germany.

A Netherlands side featuring Ruud Gullit, Frank Rijkaard and Marco van Basten won the country's first ever major championship in 1988.

In 1976, Wales made it through their group into the knock-out stages for the only time in their history. They then lost to Yugoslavia.

In 2012, Spain became the first team in the history of the tournament to win back-to-back trophies.

Portugal are perhaps the most unlucky side in European Championship history. They've made it at least as far as the semi-finals four times, but never won the trophy.

In 2000, Yugoslavia drew 3–3 with Slovenia in the group stage, despite having Siniša Mihajlović dismissed on the hour. They were trailing 3–0 at the time.

The most goals ever scored by a single player in one tournament stands at nine – and the honour goes to France's Michel Platini, who was in red-hot form during the 1984 championship, staged in his home country.

The Soviet Union reached three successive European Championship finals in the 1980s – and lost every one!

A whopping eight players have notched hat-tricks in a European Championship final, including Frenchman Michel Platini (twice), Dutchman Patrick Kluivert and Spaniard David Villa.

QUICK OFF THE MARK

The fastest-ever goal scored in the European Championship was notched by Russia's Dmitri Kirichenko against Greece in 2004 after just 68 seconds.

Dutch stopper Edwin van der Sar went an incredible 12 years without conceding a goal in this tournament – racking up nine clean sheets between 1996 and 2008.

The 1960 final kicked off at 10 p.m. local time on a Sunday evening. By the time Soviet Union striker Victor Ponedelnik, whose surname translates as 'Monday', notched the extra-time winner, it was already Monday in the USSR.

Greece's Giorgos Karagounis holds the dubious honour of being the dirtiest player in European Championship history. He was booked eight times across three tournaments between 2004 and 2012.

Velcro-gloved stopper Francesco Toldo kept out three penalties in Italy's semi-final triumph against the Netherlands in 2000.

The 1992 winners Denmark weren't even supposed to be in the tournament. They only qualified at the last minute due to the war breaking out in Yugoslavia, which saw the eastern European country disqualified. As the runner up in their qualifying group, Denmark stepped in – and the rest is history.

TIKI-TAKA!

When Spain beat Ireland in 2012, La Roja made a whopping 810 completed passes compared to their opponents' 198. The catalyst? Engine-room stoker Xavi, who racked up 127 himself – a record in a 90-minute European Championship encounter.

Spain have only ever failed to qualify for the European Championship on one occasion – back in 1992.

The first ever European Championship final in 1960 was refereed by an Englishman – Arthur Ellis – who took care of the whistle as Soviet Union beat Yugoslavia 2–1 at Parc des Princes, Paris.

Before the 1964 final, Spain manager José Villalonga drew out a pitch in the sand around the Bernabéu Stadium pitch, and used stones to represent his players, using pine cones for the opposition. Stones, he said, were stronger. His side went on to win 2–1.

On 18 June 1972, West Germany strolled to a 3–0 victory in the final against Soviet Union, and it was the start of a dominance which lasted over two decades. The Germans went on to reach nine of the next 13 major tournament finals.

Greece reached their first major tournament in the 1980 finals, and wouldn't appear in another European Championship until 2004 – when they won the trophy.

In 2012, Spain's moustachioed maestro Vicente del Bosque became the first coach in history to win the European Championship, World Cup and European Cup.

When Croatia's Ivan Klasnić scored in his country's win against Poland in 2008, the goal meant more than most. It came just 18 months after the player underwent two kidney transplants – the first donation, from his mother, was rejected, but the second, from his father, provided a match.

ORANGE AND OVERJOYED

When the Netherlands booked their place in the final with a 2–1 victory over Germany in 1988, the celebrations that followed were the largest public gathering in the country since the events that marked the end of World War Two. The Dutchmen went on lift the trophy after beating the Soviet Union 2–0.

Spoon-bending paranormalist Uri Geller famously claimed that his magical mind-powers had caused the ball to move just before Gary McAllister's missed penalty in Scotland's 2–0 loss to England in 1996.

ON ME HEAD, SON!

Out of 76 goals notched at Euro 2012, a record 22 were headers, including Robert Lewandowski's opening-game notch against Greece – the first goal of the finals.

EURO BIG HITTERS - THE MOST GOALS SCORED

Player	Goals	Championships
Michel Platini (FRA)	9 goals in 5 games	1972–1987
Alan Shearer (ENG)	7 goals in 9 games	1988–2006
Ruud van Nistelrooy (NED)	6 goals in 8 games	1993–2012
Patrick Kluivert (NED)	6 goals in 9 games	1994–2008
Zlatan Ibrahimović (SWE)	6 goals in 10 games	1999–present
Thierry Henry (FRA)	6 goals in 11 games	1994–2014
Cristiano Ronaldo (POR)	6 goals in 14 games	2002–present
Nuno Gomes (POR)	6 goals in 14 games	1994–2013
Savo Milošević (SER)	5 goals in 4 games	1992–2008
Wayne Rooney (ENG)	5 goals in 6 games	2002–present

EURO CHAMPIONSHIP TROPHY WINS

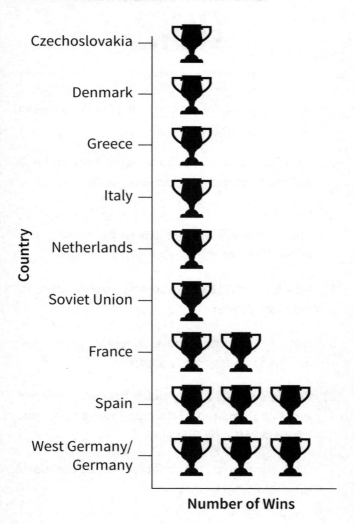

Number of Wins

THE EUROPEAN CHAMPIONSHIP
QUIZ

----

1) When and where was the first ever European Championship played?

2) **How many nations have won back-to-back European Championship trophies?**

3) Who became the youngest player in European Championship history when he turned out against Denmark in 2012?

4) **Why was the 1992 European Championship in Sweden unique?**

5) How many times have England lifted the European Championship trophy?

6) **France's Michel Platini holds the record for the most goals scored in a single tournament, but how many did he bang in?**

7) Who pioneered the concept of a European Championship tournament?

8) **Dutch keeper Edwin van der Sar and French defender Lilian Thuram share a European Championship record – but what is it?**

9) Which country will host the 2016 European Championship?

10) **In 2004, at 19 years and 150 days, Portugal's Cristiano Ronaldo became the youngest player to turn out in a European Championship final – but who did his team face?**

11) West Germany's Rainer Bonhof appeared in three consecutive European Championship finals – but which ones?

12) **Austria's Ivica Vastic holds a European Championship record – but what is it?**

13) England's 1996 official European Championship song, 'Three Lions', has sold over one million copies since it was released – but which two comedians wrote and performed it?

14) **The Bernabéu Stadium was packed with 79,115 spectators for the 1964 final – but which two teams contested it?**

15) Russia's Dmitri Kirichenko was quick out of the blocks in the 2004 tournament and notched the fastest goal in tournament history – but how quick was he?

STADIUMS

> *Wembley is the cathedral of football. It is the capital of football and it is the heart of football.*
>
> **PELÉ**

It's over 120 years since England saw the rise of its first purpose-built football stadium, Everton's Goodison Park. In the time since, it's fair to say that humans have grown rather proficient at designing and building some stunning sports arenas around the world. But it's not just about feats of engineering. These awesome structures hold many memories, dreams and ideals for players, managers and supporters alike.

There's Liverpool's Anfield, famous for its electric atmosphere on European nights, with the Kop throbbing and in full voice.

There's Old Trafford, Manchester United's 'Theatre of Dreams', a place full of fear for visiting sides desperate to put in a good performance in front of the Stretford End.

And further afield, the likes of the Allianz Arena, Camp Nou and the Maracana, which packed in over 200,000 fans for the 1950 World Cup final – still the highest attendance in history.

These places are as much a part of any club as the players, manager or badge. For many fans, the click of the turnstile, the buzz of the crowd and the smell of the hallowed turf is an almost spiritual experience. If football is a religion, then these places, big and small, old and new, are the temples where we worship.

Separated by just 250 yards, Dundee and Dundee United's grounds, Dens Park and Tannadice Park, are geographically the closest professional football stadiums in the UK.

Between 2000 and 2006, Austrian side Sturm Graz's ground was called the Arnold Schwarzenegger Stadium. They're not sure what's so special about it – but if you go there once, you'll be back.

The Eidi Stadium in the Faroe Islands couldn't be any closer to the Atlantic – it's flanked on two sides by the ocean. It's freezing cold, windy and if you shank your shot you'll be swapping your boots for a wetsuit to fetch the ball.

DID YOU KNOW?

The highest attendance at any football game ever was recorded at the 1950 World Cup final between Brazil and Uruguay, as 173,850 fans crammed into the Maracana in Rio de Janeiro – and many estimate that the unofficial total was nearer to 200,000.

The last ever England international at the old Wembley in 2000 saw the Three Lions lose 1–0 against the old rivals, Germany.

During the opening ceremony of the 1994 World Cup in USA, Diana Ross took to the Soldier Field pitch in Chicago to sing a few songs. As part of her performance, she had to bury a close-range penalty, which would trigger a huge ticker-tape parade.

Unfortunately, Diana didn't have her scoring boots on – and hit her shot wide of the target. Nevertheless, the goal still snapped in two, releasing thousands of white balloons and glitter fountains.

TRULY TOP-TIER FOOTBALL

How do you fancy getting to the ground by cable car? That's what the players at the Ottmar Hitzfeld Stadium in Switzerland have to do. At 2,000 metres above sea level, it's carved into the Zermatt mountains – the highest ground in Europe.

Arbroath's Gayfield Park is the closest stadium to the sea in the whole of Europe. A word of advice: if it's windy, avoid the East Stand – the waves have been known to wash over the wall!

In January 1922 the Duke of York, later King George VI, cut the first turf to mark the beginning of the erection of Wembley Stadium – and it was completed in less than a year at a cost of £750,000.

Opened in 1855, Sheffield United's Bramall Lane is the oldest major stadium in the world still hosting professional football matches.

Coventry City's Highfield Road was the first stadium to be converted from standing terraces to an all-seater stadium in 1981.

Since the 1980s, Everton has allowed supporters' ashes to be buried around the perimeter of their Goodison Park pitch.

When Southampton's St Mary's Stadium was constructed in the early 2000s, sneaky fans of local rivals Portsmouth are said to have buried Pompey memorabilia in strategic places – including a shrine buried under the centre circle.

In a 1998 clash between South African teams Moroka Swallows and Jomo Cosmos, a blast of lightning struck the pitch, sending players and supporters from both sides scattering. Two Swallows players were kept in hospital with their injuries, and the game was abandoned.

The stadium with the largest capacity in the world is the Rungrado May Day Stadium in North Korea, which can contain a whopping 150,000 spectators.

England's national stadium, Wembley, was demolished in 2003 and took four years to rebuild, at a cost of nearly £800 million. The first competitive fixture at the new 90,000-seater stadium was Stevenage Borough v Kidderminster Harriers in the final of the FA Trophy on 12 May 2007.

Estadio Hernando Siles in Bolivia is home to three clubs – Club Bolivar, La Paz and The Strongest. It's also one of the highest professional football stadiums in the world, at a whopping 3,637 metres above sea level. It's often been claimed that the lack of oxygen gives the Bolivian national team an advantage on home soil.

Borussia Dortmund's Westfalenstadion is renowned as being one of the most atmospheric in world football. The *Südtribüne*, or South Stand, is the largest terrace for standing spectators in European football, and is regularly full to its 24,454 capacity.

GHOSTS BEHIND THE GOALPOSTS?

Many believe that FC Porto's Estádio do Dragão is haunted. In a 2012 Champions League match between FC Porto and Paris Saint-Germain, a cameraman who captured the celebration of a goal by the home side's James Rodriguez also recorded the presence of a spirit among the fans who were celebrating in the stands. The spirit seemed to be excited with the goal as well – a half smile showing on his spectral face.

Moscow's Luzhniki Stadium was one of the first European stadia to install artificial turf, a move which was approved by FIFA in 2002 due to the harsh Russian winters.

During a 1–1 bore draw with Burnley in 2013, a Blackburn Rovers fan released a chicken on to the Ewood Park pitch in protest at the club's owners, Venky's, an Indian company specialising in chicken processing. It took several stewards and a pair of players what seemed like an eternity to catch the plucky imposter, and the game was delayed by several minutes while it gave them the run around.

BEST STADIUM ANNOUNCEMENTS

'The next match here at the Banks's Stadium is on New Year's Day, which this year falls on 1 January.'

Walsall announcer at halftime against Millwall.

'There's a no-smoking policy in all parts of the Layer Road ground. Anyone who is caught smoking will be taken away, strapped to an electric chair and electrocuted until they are dead. Thank you.'

Colchester announcer at halftime against Leicester.

'Please stand for the national anthem of the Republic of Northern Ireland.'

The St Mary's stadium announcer gets mixed up before the start of the England Under-21 international with the Republic of Ireland.

'Can the people trying to break into the boardroom please be aware you are on CCTV.'

Mansfield stadium announcer after the Stags lost to Rotherham.

'His wife always dreamed of a hunky fireman, but all she got was a chunky tyre-man.'

Announcer at Manchester United, introducing one of the participants in the halftime penalty shoot-out.

'And now the Olympiacos team sheet... wish me luck!'

Chelsea announcer before reading out a list of players including Żewłakow, Patsatzoglou and Djordjevic.

'There's a mustard-coloured Peugeot in the car park. You've left your windows open. Chances are if your car is a mustard colour you want it to be nicked, but just to let you know.'

Announcer before the Plymouth v Burnley match.

'If there is a qualified referee in the ground, please can he make himself known to a steward.'

Halftime at Fulham v Middlesbrough after a few questionable decisions.

'Mr Coombes in L1, your wife has just gone into labour.'

At Leicester v Barnsley.

'The scorer for Belper... someone wearing a yellow shirt.'

Baffled stadium announcer during a match between Colwyn Bay v Belper Town.

'In case you didn't hear the score from earlier today – St Mirren 1, Celtic didnae.'

Stadium announcer in Hearts v Partick fixture.

'Would the owner of car registration number XXXX XXX, please return immediately to your vehicle, as it's on fire!'

Stadium announcer in a Peterborough v Millwall clash.

STADIUMS
QUIZ

----

1) How did the Luzhniki Stadium in Moscow make history?

2) **If you were jumping up and down in the Südtribüne, which club would you be supporting?**

3) True or false – there is more leg room in every seat at the new Wembley than there was in the royal box of the old Wembley?

4) **Which English stadium was severely damaged by fire back in 1985?**

5) Why might you feel a little queasy at the Faroe Island's Eidi Stadium?

6) **There were 39 of these previously, and now there are 107. What am I talking about?**

7) I'm stood outside of Roots Hall. Which club's home ground am I about to enter?

8) **In 2011, US President Barack Obama presented one architect with a prize for his pioneering design of a European club's stadium – but which club was it?**

9) What is the estimated cost of FC Bayern Munich's incredible Allianz Arena? Is it $100 million, $200 million or $400 million?

10) **Which stadium is commonly known as the 'Theatre of Dreams'?**

11) Just 250 yards separates the stadiums of two British football clubs – which clubs are they?

12) **What is the oldest continually used football stadium in the world, having welcomed spectators since 1875?**

13) Which stadium has the largest capacity in the world, at a whopping 150,000?

14) **Which was the first British football ground to be converted to an all-seater stadium, back in 1981?**

15) Which club plays at the Etihad Stadium?

TRANSFERS

> *Do you think I'd enter into a contract with that mob? Absolutely no chance. I wouldn't sell them a virus. That's a 'no' by the way. There's no agreement whatsoever between the clubs.*

ALEX FERGUSON ON RUMOURS LINKING CRISTIANO RONALDO TO REAL MADRID IN 2009

A super yacht. Nine sprawling Manhattan townhouses. Over 700 Ferrari Californias.

Nope, it's not the best episode of the *Generation Game* ever – that's just what Real Madrid could have bought with the £86 million that they spent on Gareth Bale in 2013.

They say that money makes the world go round, and that's never been more true than in the world of twenty-first century, top-level football. At the turn of every transfer window, twice a year, the rumour mill clicks slowly into action – agents come, rubbing their eyes, out of hibernation, players begin to flash their knickers and chairmen dust off the chequebooks.

In truth, it's become something of a pantomime. Long gone are the days when a transfer would be sealed with a handshake over a cup of tea in the boardroom. These days, multi-million-pound switches can take weeks or even months to come to fruition. It's all about the contract, the salary negotiations, image rights, sell-on clauses and bonuses.

Football is business – and a lucrative one at that. But not all players go for big money. In fact, as you're about to read, historically, some transfer fees have been a lot more imaginative than that…

The summer of 1966 was a big one for England star Alan Ball. After winning the World Cup on home turf, he moved from Blackpool to Everton in August for a record transfer fee between British clubs: £110,000. Upon signing for the Toffees, he received a phone call from Liverpool boss Bill Shankly, who said, 'Never mind, Alan. At least you'll be able to play next to a great team!'

When Garforth Town announced in 2004 that they had signed Brazilian legend Socrates, few people could believe it. How could this classic playmaker, captain of the great Brazilian side from the 1982 World Cup, wash up in West Yorkshire? Fifty-year-old Socrates made his debut against Tadcaster United in front of a crowd of 1,300 fans. He played 12 minutes as a substitute – but it turned out to be his only appearance for the Miners, claiming that it was far too cold for his liking.

David Beckham's 2006 move to Major League Soccer shocked the world, but it's estimated that, through his salary, revenue-sharing and endorsements, he pocketed a whopping $255 million (£163 million) during his six years at LA Galaxy.

HE TALKS A GOOD GAME...

Ali Dia, or 'Ali Dire', as many Saints fans now call him, got in touch with Southampton boss Graeme Souness in 1996 in what remains one of the cheekiest transfers ever. After the player claimed he was the cousin of African superstar George Weah (he wasn't), and that he'd won 13 international caps (he hadn't), the Saints snapped him up and thrust him straight into the first-team squad. After coming on as a substitute, the crowd had to endure 50 miserable minutes before the player was hauled off and disappeared into obscurity.

In the summer of 2014, Manchester United smashed all incoming British transfer records when they snapped up Real Madrid's Ángel Di María for a stunning £59.7 million.

When Italian giants AC Milan surprisingly shelled out £1 million on Watford striker Luther Blissett in 1983, the Vicarage Road player jumped at the chance of a San Siro move. However, just a year later, after five goals in 30 appearances, he was on his way back to

England. The story goes that the Rossoneri actually meant to sign his Hornets teammate John Barnes all along.

Manchester United paid Middlesbrough a British record fee of £2.3 million for tough defender Gary Pallister in 1989. But the chunky price tag was worlds away from his previous move, when Boro snaffled him from non-league Billingham Town for just a few kits, a ball and a set of goal nets five years earlier!

In the summer of 1998, West Ham defender David Unsworth moved to Aston Villa for £3 million. Less than a month later, before the season had even kicked off, he was off again – heading to Everton – and said that his family was unable to settle in Birmingham.

ALL IN A DAY'S WORK

Footballers haven't always been raking it in. In the 1940s, England star Tom Finney would often arrive at games with his plumbing tools in a wheelbarrow, rip teams apart for 90 minutes, and then head off to finish a job!

In 2014, FC Barcelona were banned from signing any new players in 2015 following a breach of rules around signing international under-18 players.

In February 2013, desperate for a move away from West Bromwich Albion, Nigerian international Peter Odemwingie decided to take matters into his own hands. He packed his bags and drove 125 miles to Queens Park Rangers – only to be told that no deal had been agreed between the two clubs, and his arrival in London had rather embarrassingly been caught by TV cameras. He returned to the Midlands 24 hours later and managed another seven months at the Hawthorns before eventually being shipped out to Cardiff City by boss Steve Clark.

Everton legend Dixie Dean moved to the Toffees  from Tranmere Rovers for just £3,000 in 1925. He went on to notch 383 goals in 433 games, which might just make him one of the biggest bargains of all time.

Diego Maradona is so good that he's the only player in history to smash the world transfer record twice. Barcelona paid £3 million for him in 1982, and Napoli coughed up £5 million three years later.

Paris Saint-Germain's iconic forward Zlatan Ibrahimović is the player who has racked up the highest cumulative transfer fees in football history. His moves from Malmö to France via Ajax, Juventus, Inter Milan, Barcelona and AC Milan have cost his employers £150 million in total.

The current transfer window system was introduced by FIFA in 2002–03. The summer window runs from June to the end of August/early September, and the winter window re-opens across most major leagues in Europe on New Year's Day, running for a month.

In 2013, Welsh wizard Gareth Bale became the first player in history to move for a fee in excess of €100 million, when he switched from Tottenham Hotspur to Real Madrid.

CATCH THAT!

Gianluigi Buffon became the most expensive goalie of all time when he moved from Parma to Juventus for a massive £30 million in 2001.

The Bosman Ruling wasn't introduced until 1995, when Belgian footballer Jean-Marc Bosman took his club to court, accusing them of preventing him from joining a new side. A landmark judgement ruled in his favour, allowing professional players in the EU to move freely at the end of their contract – and it changed the footballing landscape forever.

English clubs splashed out the most money in the summer 2014 transfer window – a whopping £857 million, dwarfing the next highest amount, £425 million, in Spain.

When Darlington chairman George Reynolds paraded 'new signing' Colombian legend Faustino Asprilla on the Feethams pitch in 2002, fans of the then English Fourth Division club could be forgiven for rubbing their eyes in disbelief. If they doubted the validity of the surprise move, they were right – the South American swiftly disappeared before putting pen to paper, never to return to the north east. The South American later claimed that promises were broken by the Quakers.

Pelé, the most celebrated player ever, came out of retirement in 1975 to sign for New York Cosmos. As the star attraction in the North American Soccer League, his first appearance drew a capacity 22,500 crowd, with a further 50,000 fans locked out.

BECAUSE THEY'RE WORTH IT!

THE STRANGEST TRANSFER FEES IN FOOTBALL HISTORY

In 1927, Manchester United boss Herbert Bamlett snapped up Stockport County defender Hugh McLenahan in exchange for two freezers full of ice cream.

When Norwegian striker Kenneth Kristensen scored a move from Vindbjart to Floey in 2002, his new club paid for the forward in shrimps – namely, his bodyweight in shrimps. The fee was measured out in a boxing-style weigh in.

In 1921, Hull City snapped up Barnsley-born Ernie Blenkinsop from amateur side Cudworth Village Club FC for just £100 and a barrel of beer! He went on to secure 26 England caps and a pair of Football League titles in an illustrious career. Cheers to that!

Arsenal legend Ian Wright went on to become one of the most feared strikers in Premier League history – but in 1985, he moved from Greenwich Borough to Crystal Palace for a set of weights.

In 1988, Chesterfield signed lumbering striker Andy Morris from local rivals Rotherham United for the bargain fee of £500 and a bag of balls. The forward went on to notch 56 goals in 225 appearances for the Spireites.

THE ONLY WAY IS UP – THE EVOLUTION OF TRANSFER FEES

First three-figure transfer fee
Willie Groves
£100 to Aston Villa, 1893

First four-figure transfer fee
Alf Common
£1,000 to Middlesbrough, 1905

First five-figure transfer fee
David Jack
£10,890 to Arsenal, 1928

First six-figure transfer fee
Luis Suárez
£1 million to Inter Milan, 1961

First seven-figure transfer fee
Jean-Pierre Papin
£10 million to AC Milan, 1992

Biggest ever transfer
Gareth Bale
£85.3 million to Real Madrid, 2013

TRANSFERS
QUIZ

---

1) In 1995, an England international striker hit the headlines when he made a £15 million switch to his hometown club from Blackburn Rovers. Who was he?

2) **From which club did Manchester United sign record capture Ángel di María?**

3) Flamboyant Swede Zlatan Ibrahimović is the most expensive player of all-time, with cumulative transfer fees totaling £150 million. Which seven clubs has he played for?

4) **One player was so good that FC Barcelona and Napoli saw fit to twice break the transfer record to sign him. Who was he?**

5) The transfer of Trevor Francis from Birmingham City to Nottingham Forest is famous for what reason?

6) **In July 2015, Southampton decided to cut their losses and cancelled the contract of their £14.6 million flop record signing. Who was he?**

7) Which lower league club did a fresh-faced David Beckham turn out for, on loan from Manchester United?

8) **How much money did English clubs splash out in the summer 2014 transfer window? Was it £248 million, £540 million or £857 million?**

9) How did Ali Dia manage to bluff his way to a Premier League appearance?

10) **Aston Villa made football history when they splashed out on Willie Groves in 1893. How much did they sign him for?**

11) Which Brazilian became the most expensive defender in history when he moved from Chelsea to Paris Saint-Germain for a massive £50 million in the summer of 2014?

12) **Italian maestro Andrea Pirlo raised eyebrows in the summer of 2015 when he moved from Juventus to which club?**

13) Arsenal hotshot Ian Wright was bought for a unique transfer fee by Crystal Palace. What was it?

14) **In 2013, Real Madrid recorded a world-record transfer fee when they captured the signature**

of Welsh winger Gareth Bale for €100 million.
Who did they sign him from?

15) When Manchester United signed Southampton's
Luke Shaw for £30 million in 2014, he became
the most expensive teenager in history. Who
held the record previously?

GOALIES

> *Somewhere in there, the grace of a ballet dancer joins with the strength of an SAS squaddie, the dignity of an ancient king, and the nerve of a bomb disposal officer.*

EAMON DUNPHY

Ah, goalkeepers. They're, um, different, aren't they? According to the old saying, 'They're all crazy, it's just that some are crazier than others'. OK – maybe crazy is a bit strong. But there's no denying that the men between the sticks are some of the game's most interesting and flamboyant characters. It's a lonely position, keeping goal, but one which has long fascinated football fans, as suggested by the number of goalkeepers with a nickname on the terraces.

There's the Iron Curtain (Russia's Rinat Dasaev), the Always-Standing Little Hercules (Italian Aldo Olivieri), the Elastic Wonder (Argentina's Ángel Bossio), the Ballet Dancer with the Hands of Steel (Yugoslavia's Vladimir Beara).

There's the Cat of Prague (Czech Republic's František Plánička), the Cat of the Maracana (Spaniard Antoni Ramallets), the Black Panther (Soviet Union's Lev Yashin), the Black Spider (Soviet Union's Lev Yashin), and the Black Octopus (er, Soviet Union's Lev Yashin again).

These alter egos suggest mythical, perhaps even superheroic, qualities on the part of the gloved wonders – rescuing points, saving sure-fire goals, defying gravity. The quirky nature of goalkeepers will never change, and that's what makes tales from the goalmouth some of the best in the game.

Did you know that Harry Rennie, who kept goal for Scottish club Greenock Morton in the late 1800s, toughened up by launching himself on to wooden boards for up to an hour each day? Or that John Burridge, who played for 29 clubs across Britain before retiring at the ripe old age of 46, used to ask his wife to launch fruit at him when he wasn't looking in order to sharpen up his reflexes?

At school, no one wanted to go in goal, because ultimately, the buck stops with the goalkeeper. You could spend 89 minutes pouncing on goal-pestering strikers, shutting out world-class attacks. But misread the flight of a single shot, fail to spot a divot, or blunder a butter-fingered ball into the net, and you'd become the scapegoat. What kind of person would choose a job like that?

Welcome to the goalmouth. Let's just say that, crazy or not, you *do* have to be a little bit mad to work here.

With just 17 minutes to go in the 1956 FA Cup final, Manchester City keeper Bert Trautmann suffered an injury following a collision with Birmingham's Peter Murphy. After a lengthy stoppage, the German goalie played on in agony, making two key saves as his side clinched a 3–1 victory. It was only days later that a scan revealed he'd broken a bone in his neck.

> *'If you're a goalkeeper, it doesn't matter what you save the ball with – if you keep it out, it's not a goal.'*

Mark Lawrenson

The men between the sticks have a reputation for being a little, well, rotund. None more so than Sheffield United keeper Billy 'Fatty' Foulkes, who at one point in his career weighed over 20 stone.

Argentinian goalie Amadeo Carrizo is widely regarded as the first stopper to use gloves, whilst playing for River Plate in the 1940s and 1950s.

England's Gordon Banks, one of the best keepers of all time, only started using goalie gloves as an experiment in the 1970 World Cup – and went on to make one of the most famous saves in history, denying Pelé a near-certain goal.

After fracturing his skull against Reading in 2006, Chelsea's Petr Cech has worn a padded, protective helmet on the field ever since.

GREEN-FINGERED GOALIES

Until the mid-1970s, many goalkeepers only wore gloves in wet conditions. Indeed, the lack of specialist goalie-glove manufacturers meant that some of the era's best goalies just used standard gardening gloves.

'Everybody makes mistakes, but when goalkeepers make them, it is costly. That's the nature of being a goalkeeper.'

Gary Speed

In 1924, Manchester City keeper Jim Mitchell became the first and only man to play for England wearing glasses, when he was capped against Ireland.

Queen of the South goalkeeper Willie Fotheringham actually left his false teeth in the back of his net following a game away to Arbroath. The gnashers were returned via a fish delivery lorry the following week.

At the age of 38 years and 232 days, Germany goalkeeper Jens Lehmann became the oldest player ever to appear in the European Championship final when Germany lost to Spain in 2008.

In April 2015, Blackpool's hapless Joe Lewis signed a jersey to give to a young fan – only to be told by his struggling club that they couldn't afford another. He was forced to play the first half of their 1–1 stalemate against Reading with his own scribble on his chest.

'Football is a fertility festival. Eleven sperm trying to get into the egg. I feel sorry for the goalkeeper.'

Björk

West Brom keeper John Osborne's nickname was Bionic as he had a plastic knuckle – but this didn't prevent him from winning the FA and League Cup with the Baggies during the 1960s.

Colombian keeper Rene Higuita famously performed the 'scorpion kick' on the biggest stage of all – against England at Wembley Stadium in 1995. The brave trick was rated as one of the top 100 sporting moments of all time.

HAIR TODAY...

Bulgarian international Borislav Mikhailov gained notoriety during the 1994 World Cup when he suddenly appeared with a full head of hair having been completely bald just weeks before. It turned out that he had decided to wear a wig to help promote his toupee company back home.

In June 2014, Colombia's Faryd Mondragón became the World Cup's oldest ever player after a late sentimental substitution saw him replace David Ospina against Japan. The goalie, who appeared at six World Cups, was 43 years and three days old.

Everton's American star stopper Tim Howard famously suffers from Tourette's syndrome.

Irish keeper Tom Farquharson, who helped Cardiff City to their 1927 FA Cup triumph, supposedly always carried a handgun in his kitbag. Well, would you dare to score past him?

Leicester City's ex-Chelsea and Australian international stopper Mark Schwarzer has worn the same pair of shin pads since he was six years old.

'The conditions you need to be a good goalkeeper are exactly the same conditions you need to be a good sculptor. You must have a very good connection, in both professions, with time and space.'

Eduardo Chillida

YOU CAN TAKE THE MAN OUT OF THE VALLEYS...

Stoke City's Welsh goalie Leigh Richmond Roose was very superstitious, and always wore his lucky shirt – an old Aberystwyth jersey, which was reportedly never washed.

One keeper with a superstitious streak was Manchester United and England's Gary Bailey, who readily admits to using juju – an African form of black magic – during his 1988–90 spell with South African side Kaiser Chiefs. There must have been something in it as they won every domestic trophy while Bailey was in goal.

'It can be a lonely world as a goalkeeper.'

Hope Solo

Sao Paulo's stopper Rogério Ceni has smashed over 100 goals in his career – all from free kicks and penalties. He's the first goalie to reach that milestone, and probably the last.

Before his murder in a bar fight in 1971, Ghana's Robert Mensah was a flamboyant goalie who wasn't averse to mocking opponents by reading a newspaper while the game was in full flow. He was also known to don an over-sized flat cap to put strikers off, and get into scraps with anyone who tried to remove it.

'The joy of seeing Yuri Gagarin flying in space is only superseded by the joy of a good penalty save.'

Lev Yashin

Poor old Nicky Salapu, of American Samoa, holds the record for the most goals shipped in a game – 31. His country was handed the humiliating result by Australia in an April 2001 World Cup qualifier.

Newcastle United's slick-haired Dutch stopper Tim Krul became the first goalkeeper to be brought on specifically for a penalty shoot-out when he entered the field of play during the Netherlands' 2014 World Cup quarter-final game against Costa Rica in the last minute. He saved two penalties and his side went on to win the shoot-out 4–3.

THE CLEANEST SHEET

Brazilian Matos Filho Mazarópi went a massive 1,816 minutes without conceding a goal for Vasco da Gama between May 1977 and September 1978.

Stoke City's Asmir Begović scored after just 12 seconds during the Potters' Premier League clash against Southampton in November 2013. It is believed to be the quickest goal ever scored by a goalkeeper.

Paraguayan stopper José Luis Chilavert became the first keeper to notch a hat-trick in November 1999, when he dispatched three spot kicks for Vélez Sarsfield against Ferro Carril Oeste.

GOALIES
QUIZ

---

1) Who is the only goalkeeper ever to receive the prestigious Ballon d'Or?

2) **Why does Nicky Salapu hate the number 31?**

3) Which goalie became the oldest player ever to appear in a European Championship Final in 2008?

4) **Brazilian Rogério Ceni holds a unique footballing record – but why?**

5) Why did Manchester City stopper Bert Trautman gain renown in the 1956 FA Cup final?

6) **Which keeper holds the record for the most international clean sheets over the course of his career?**

7) Which crazy Colombian shocked the world with a scorpion kick during a routine friendly against England in 1995?

8) **Portuguese keeper Ricardo made the headlines in the 2004 penalty shoot-out against England – but why?**

9) Why did Paraguayan José Luis Chilavert have a game to remember against Ferro Carril Oeste in 1999?

10) **Italian keeper Gianluigi Buffon holds a special World Cup record. What is it?**

11) Multicoloured jerseys were the norm for this South American in the early 1990s – but who is he?

12) **True or false – the original laws of the game permitted goalkeepers to handle the ball anywhere in their half of the pitch?**

13) Which keeper racked up the most penalty saves during his Premier League career?

14) **As of 2015, who is the most expensive keeper of all-time?**

15) Argentina's Amadeo Carrizo played an integral part in the evolution of goalkeeping performance – but why?

FOOTIE FASHION

> **In terms of Liverpool's reputation, never has so much damage been done. The Spice Boys had been born.**
>
> DOMINIC MATTEO ON LIVERPOOL'S HORRIFIC 1995 FA CUP FINAL SUITS

Football and fashion. They go together like a His and Hers customised, designer Italian leather washbag and luggage set. From the turf to the terraces, these two iconic industries collide day in, day out. The result? A multi-million-dollar business.

But it hasn't always been this way. In fact, football kits as we know them today weren't even introduced until less than a century ago – and the sale of replica kits and memorabilia even more recently.

It all started with George Best – the 'fifth Beatle' – back in the swinging sixties. Stylish, slick and sexy, his appeal transcended the sport in the way that Cristiano Ronaldo and Neymar do today.

Since then, the likes of Kevin Keegan, Johan Cruyff and David Beckham have all successfully made the leap to the catwalk, launching their own fashion lines and embracing all that the industry has to offer.

As is so often the case in football these days, talent brings money – but money doesn't bring taste. Just ask Mario Balotelli, if you ever see him climb out of his camouflage-print super car.

But it's not just about style – it's about superstition too. For example, did you know that ex-England midfielder Paul Ince was so paranoid of attracting bad luck that he would refuse to don his jersey until he was out of the tunnel? Or that Manchester United once scrapped their brand new grey kit at half time because the players claimed that they couldn't see each other on the pitch?

And the wacky ideas keep on coming. In just the last couple of years we've had 'invisible' grass-printed football boots, sickness-inducing garish kit designs and even the explosion of thermal snoods and tights across the Premier League.

One thing's for sure – the relationship between these two big businesses isn't going to end anytime soon. And, as long as the beautiful game remains more about trophies than trends, and cups than couture, that's fine by me.

The first time that official football kits were used was in 1928, when Chelsea faced Arsenal.

As of 2015, Manchester United's £53-million-per-year sponsorship deal with US car giant Chevrolet is the biggest in football history.

Pelé once dispatched a friend to track down a fan to whom the Brazil legend had given one of his playing shirts, with orders to retrieve it at all costs, after suffering a dip in form. A week later the friend handed Pelé his shirt back, and the striker's form immediately returned.

Cristiano Ronaldo is so superstitious that he insists on being the only Portuguese national team player who may start off a game wearing a long-sleeved jersey.

Boca Juniors couldn't decide which shirt colours to use so one day in 1907 they decided that they were going to pick the colours from the first ship to arrive in the harbour the next day. The first ship was a Swedish ship so they picked the colours blue and yellow from the Swedish flag.

DID YOU KNOW?

Juventus and Notts County might seem poles apart, but they have a lot more in common that you'd think. In fact, the Italian giants only wear their famous black and white stripes because a friend of ex-player John Savage sent them a set of Notts County kits back in 1903!

Pelé and the famous number 10 shirt go back a long way. It was during the World Cup of 1954 that players began to keep the same shirt number – and many did so throughout the whole tournament.

When Scottish club Queen's Park was founded in 1867, the only piece of kit that was consistent across every player was an armband.

England captain Bobby Moore insisted on being the last player in the changing rooms to put on his shorts before kick-off. His teammate, Martin Peters, would tease the defender by removing his shorts at the last moment – to which Moore would respond by removing his, too.

Blue is the team colour of one of the most stylish nations in football, Italy. It dates back to the association of the colour with the royal dynasty that unified Italy in 1861. One of the favourite chants of the Italian faithful is *'Forza Azzurri!'*, which translates as 'Blue Power!'

In 2012, Denmark striker Nicklas Bendtner was fined a whopping £80,000 and banned for a game for revealing sponsored boxer shorts after scoring against Portugal in the European Championship.

Football goalies didn't have to wear different coloured shirts from their teammates until 1913.

Spanish international striker Álvaro Negredo admitted that he always keeps the same shirt in the next match after scoring a goal – although he clarified that he washes it first.

LICENCE TO PRINT MONEY

In the late 1970s, British clubs were the first to begin selling replica team shirts in bulk, and they quickly realised that it was a goldmine.

In 1996, Manchester United unveiled a brand new grey away kit – but quickly ditched it after complaints that it made players 'invisible' to each other. It's since been voted their worst ever strip in a fans' poll.

If ex-England poacher Gary Lineker failed to notch in the first half of a game, he would change his shirt at half time.

Italian coach Renzo Ulivieri had great belief in the power of his lucky coat – even wearing it through a match in Palermo despite the temperatures exceeding 35°C.

Marseille defender Basile Boli had a pair of lucky underpants which he wore in every game, from his first professional appearance to the 1993 Champions League final in Munich. On that fateful night, his headed goal won his side the coveted trophy, so maybe there was method in his madness after all.

Ex-Spain coach Luis Aragones was so offended by the colour yellow that when star striker Raúl turned up to international duty in a canary-coloured shirt, his gaffer ordered him back to the team hotel to change.

In 2009, Newcastle United launched a new, banana-coloured away kit. It was surprisingly a hit with Toon fans – but fans of opposition clubs had a right laugh at their expense, singing 'Bananas in pyjamas are going down the league' for most of the season.

In England, players' shirts were first numbered in 1939, at the request of the Football Management Committee.

Whilst he was captain at Shakhtar Donetsk and Zenit St Petersburg, Anatoliy Tymoshchuk always wore two armbands – his own, and one that previously belonged to German midfield general Lothar Matthäus, his childhood idol.

A LOAD OF WANKAS

A Peruvian club was lost for words when thousands of orders started flooding in for their replica shirts – from the UK. A spokeseman for the club, Deportivo Wanka, shrugged, 'It is very strange. Everyone in Britain seems to think we have a funny name.'

Bosnian midfielder Bruno Akrapović had a penchant for the number 8 shirt throughout his lengthy career in Germany. The reason? He signed his first German contract – at SV Arminia Hannover – on 8 August 1988.

Niklas Bendtner asked to wear the number 52 shirt for Arsenal and Sunderland. It might seem like a weird choice from the Dane, but rumour has it that this was because he was being paid £52,000 a week. Show off!

Liverpool defender Dejan Lovren could probably knock up a pretty stylish kit given the opportunity. The Croatian international runs his own fashion line, called Russell Brown.

Two of the world's biggest football brands, Adidas and Puma, were actually started by German brothers Adi and Rudi Dassler. The pair became bitter enemies in their quest to be the number one brand in sports merchandise.

The Cameroon national side has twice been ticked off by FIFA for contravening kit laws. First, the African nation unveiled a sleeveless jersey in 2002, and then, in 2006, they turned up in an all-in-one leotard-style kit! Needless to say, you don't want to have to answer a call of nature wearing one of those.

When Chelsea goalie Petr Cech turned up in a bright orange jersey in 2008, many claimed he looked like a walking tangerine. But the keeper was unabashed, claiming that 'Studies say the orange colour spreads the most when the striker attacks, in the split of a second as he focuses'. Right you are, Pete.

FOOTIE FASHION
QUIZ

---

1) Which world-class striker has a forearm tattoo reading 'Just enough education to perform?'

2) **Why do Argentinian side Boca Juniors wear blue and yellow?**

3) Which English club did Italian giants Juventus borrow their first ever black and white striped kit from?

4) **In 1996, Manchester United changed their kit at half-time in a game with Southampton, claiming that it made their teammates 'invisible'. What colour was the offending kit?**

5) Which permed England star became famous for advertising Brut cologne back in the 1970s?

6) **Which Premier League club is currently sponsored by Emirates?**

7) Which nation unveiled a sleeveless kit back in 2002, only to be told that it wasn't allowed to be worn?

8) **A European giant broke their no shirt sponsorship rule in 2003 to display the logo of charity UNICEF. Which club was it?**

9) In what year did English clubs begin to number jerseys?

10) **Who once said, on his Manchester United contract negotiations: 'It's not the salary that's a problem, it's just the image rights that needed a little perking.'**

11) What changed for goalkeepers in 1913?

12) **In 2013, Nike became the English national team's fifth shirt manufacturer. Who are the other four?**

13) Rumour has it that Nicklas Bendtner chose to wear the number 52 at Arsenal for a very specific reason. Why was that?

14) **Why did Real Madrid switch to black shorts for just a single season, back in 1925–26?**

15) In the 1940s, a pair of German brothers set up two of the biggest sports companies in the world. What are they?

HISTORY OF SHORT SHORTS

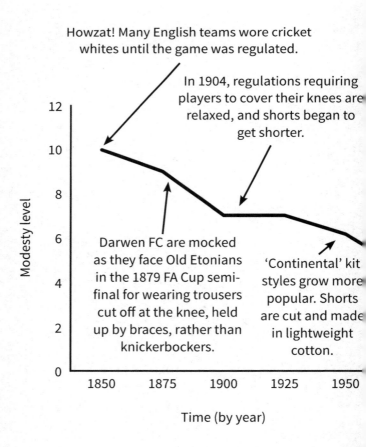

Howzat! Many English teams wore cricket whites until the game was regulated.

In 1904, regulations requiring players to cover their knees are relaxed, and shorts began to get shorter.

Darwen FC are mocked as they face Old Etonians in the 1879 FA Cup semi-final for wearing trousers cut off at the knee, held up by braces, rather than knickerbockers.

'Continental' kit styles grow more popular. Shorts are cut and made in lightweight cotton.

Modesty level

Time (by year)

[1850-2015]

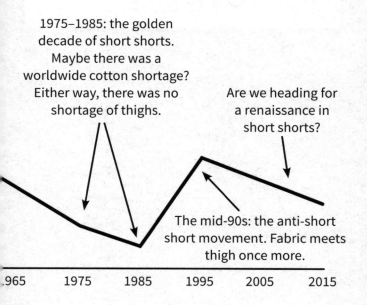

1975–1985: the golden decade of short shorts. Maybe there was a worldwide cotton shortage? Either way, there was no shortage of thighs.

Are we heading for a renaissance in short shorts?

The mid-90s: the anti-short short movement. Fabric meets thigh once more.

| .965 | 1975 | 1985 | 1995 | 2005 | 2015 |

THEY SAID WHAT?

> *For those of you watching in black and white, Spurs are in the yellow strip.*
>
> **JOHN MOTSON**

Football just wouldn't be football without pundits. And ever since the worlds of football and television collided, a good pundit has the potential to be just as entertaining to a viewer as a graceful player.

'Football punditry is an absolute art form and I'm not sure people give it enough credit,' says Sky Sports' Barney Francis. The truth is, there's football punditry, and there's bad football punditry.

And as we see more channels, and more coverage, we also see more retired players thrust in front of a camera to provide cutting-edge analysis of the 0–0 stalemate that's just rolled out in front of them.

Retired footballers who might, in a previous life, have become a pub landlord or a second-hand car salesman, now have the opportunity to become burgeoning media personalities.

And you can't blame them for grabbing the opportunity with both hands. After all, getting paid to sit around in a warm studio, watching football with your mates? Where do I sign?

Some of the corkers that these suited and booted panel experts come out with are just the equivalent of a smashed glass behind the bar or a stuttering car engine. They're a bit like Marmite, you see. We either love them, or we love to hate them. But either way, it's hard to deny that they're entertaining. So bad, they're good. Sometimes, you just can't wait to get to half time, in order to see these guys in action.

Here, I've collected some of the best gaffes from the blokes on the telly. Enjoy!

I'm not convinced that Scotland will play a typically English game.

Gareth Southgate

Most of the players will be wearing rubbers tonight.

Gary Lineker

I'd be surprised if all twenty-two players are on the field at the end of the game – one's been sent off already.

George Best

It's a football stadium in the truest sense of the word.

John Motson

Hearts are now playing with a five-man back four.

Alan McInally

The tackles are coming in thick and thin.

Alan Brazil

If Plan A fails, he could always revert to Plan A.

Mark Lawrenson

… and for those of you watching without television sets, live commentary is on Radio Two.

David Coleman

He had an eternity to play that ball, but he took too long over it.

Martin Tyler

… so different from the scenes in eighteen seventy-two, at the cup final none of us can remember.

John Motson

It's real end to end stuff but unfortunately it's all up at Forest's end.

Chris Kamara

They're the second best team in the world, and there's no higher praise than that.

Kevin Keegan

The ball came off the left breast of Sébastien Bassong.

Sam Matterface

Who'll win the league? It's a toss of a coin between three of them.

Matt Le Tissier

So this movie you star in, The Life Story of George Best. Tell us what it's about.

George Gavin

Cardiff's owner is a billionaire. He's worth about £850 million.

Ronnie Irani

It's one of them days when you just say, 'It's one of them days'.

Ian Wright

If you're going to win the Premier League, you're going to have to finish ahead of Chelsea and Man City.

Graeme Souness

From that moment, the pendulum went into reverse.

Gerald Sinstadt

The aura of uninvincibility has gone, if there is such a word.

Adrian Chiles

This is turning into a rout.

Michael Owen after Chelsea scored their sixth goal against Arsenal

It's a nightmare for strikers when defences push up. You've got to go with them or you're offside.

Michael Owen

He's a goal scorer. Not a natural-born one, not yet. That takes time.

Glenn Hoddle

MERSON'S MISHAPS

He's the ex-Arsenal and England winger who's swapped his studs for a suit and now regularly appears as a pundit on Sky Sports. His marauding style put smiles on faces during his career on the pitch, and his humour and famous word-mangling is still keeping fans entertained now he's on the sidelines. Meet Paul Merson – the man who deserves a section all of his own.

'I think Southampton will finish above teams that are well below them.'

'There's only one person gets you sacked and that's the fans.'

'They're lacking that real streak of bang.'

'When defenders get ran at they're not as great as what they are.'

'People just looked lost. Too many players looked like fish on trees.'

'In England, Rooney is a world-class footballer in the world.'

THEY SAID WHAT?

The good news for Paraguay is they've gone two-nil down so early on.

Kevin Keegan

In the end, Rosicky initially did well.

Andy Townsend

Matty Jarvis had acres of time there.

Stan Collymore

There's a snap about Liverpool that just isn't there.

Ron Atkinson

I never make predictions, and I never will.

Paul Gascoigne

He's been like a fresh of breath air.

Roy Keane

I don't want Rooney to leave these shores but if he does, I think he'll go abroad.

Ian Wright

It's an unprecedented precedent.

Clarke Carlisle

The butterflies will be jangling.

Gabby Logan

He went in with his shuds stowing.

Gary Neville

There was nothing wrong with his timing, he was just a bit late.

Mark Bright

Mistakes will be made, make no mistake.

Garth Crooks

Ramires is involved in everything he does.

Graeme Le Saux

Where do you sit on young players, Martin Keown?

Jonathan Pearce gets personal

It's pouring down and the ref is enjoying his moment in the sun.

Adrian Chiles

The half-time whistle blows and I have one word for you: Absolutely brilliant!

Sam Matterface

Most of Michael Owen's goals have come in the past.

Dan Walker

As long as you hit the target, they're going to go in... if the keeper don't make a save.

Ian Holloway

Peter Schmeichel will be like a father figure to Kasper Schmeichel.

Jamie Redknapp

These balls now – they literally explode off your feet.

Jamie Redknapp

Not many players get three cracks of the cherry.

Adrian Chiles

Everton are now hitting the ropes running.

Glenn Hoddle

Dzeko went down a bit theoretically.

Peter Reid

You need to take off your rose-scented glasses.

Robbie Savage

Plymouth Argyle haven't lost five home games in a row since December nineteen sixty-three. Oh what a night!

Jeff Stelling

Benteke have got a goalscorer in Aston Villa.

Robbie Earle

If you want to beat Burnley, you have to beat their team.

Thierry Henry

He's just thrown his head in there and it's just come off.

John Duncan

There's only one word to describe football, and that's 'if only'.

Bobby Robson

Keith Gillespie just lacks a bit of inconsistency.

Graeme Le Saux

I don't know where this arctic wind has come from, but it's freezing.

Alan Green

The offside flag went up immediately, if not before.

Jonathan Park

I know what my strengths are, and I know what my not strengths are.

Aidy Boothroyd

He's gone down like he's been felled by a tree.

Andy Gray

If they can beat Spain again, it'll be a good scalpel.

Ian Wright

I didn't say them things I said.

Glenn Hoddle

It was the perfect penalty – apart from he missed it.

Rob McCaffrey

He's gone into countless challenges, and won both of them.

Guy Mowbray

Newcastle, of course, unbeaten in their last five wins…

Alan Green

The lad got over-excited when he saw the whites of the goalpost's eyes.

Steve Coppell

Stoichkov's had a quiet game, but that's often the hallmark of greatness.

Mike Ingham

You can't do better than go away from home and get a draw…

Kevin Keegan

FUNNY OLD GAME

> *I do believe in fate.*
>
> **ALEX FERGUSON**

Fate. It's the idea that a predetermined path, or order of events, will lead to a certain outcome. It's a funny old word – just as football is a funny old game. And when you put the two together, you get a whole other phenomenon.

That's why superstition is rife in football. Players, coaches and fans all observing a series of bizarre rituals in order to try to find some spiritual sanctuary. In essence, it's all just voodoo – a desperate attempt to claw back some control of a situation that's far from controllable.

Let's face it – there are millions of variables that go into each 90-minute encounter. What did the players have to eat last night? Did the referee wake up on the wrong side of the bed? Did that butterfly's flapping wings in China spark a series of events which just caused that seemingly goal-bound ball to spin on to the post?

Some might say that any logical person would argue against the concept of fate in football. But of course, there are some footballing coincidences which just seem a little *too* perfect.

Firstly, it goes without saying that players always put in a good performance under a new manager, no matter how poor they've been for the previous six months.

When a striker misses a sitter, he nearly always limps away wincing, having sustained a mysterious injury (probably bruised pride, in most cases).

And, of course, the most certain of all situations. England will always – always – crash out of international tournaments on penalties.

So remember, as you sit down to watch your team on a Saturday afternoon, you're actually about to witness the random amalgamation of unbelievable coincidence unfold before your very eyes.

Every little twist and turn, every misplaced pass, every studs-up challenge. It's all part of the plan. Don't like it? Blame the footballing gods. And if you don't believe in all that rubbish, just blame the ref.

Here are some of the quirkiest facts, freakiest injuries and strangest coincidences from around the footballing world.

STRANGE BUT TRUE

Wrap up warm! In the winter of 1962–63, which became known as 'The Big Freeze', Halifax Town hired out their pitch as an ice rink to raise extra cash.

There's a monument in Portugal that commemorates Arsenal losing a friendly match. Back in the summer of 1948, the Gunners went on a tour of the Mediterranean country and lost to Oporto. The locals were so chuffed that they raised £20,000 to erect a permanent reminder – and it still stands today, just off the Praça de Lisboa.

West Ham and England legend Bobby Moore's middle name was Chelsea.

PASS THE SPONGE!

Birmingham City player Olivier Kapo gave an apprentice player a big thank you for cleaning his boots throughout the season – his car. The French international handed over the keys to his flash Mercedes as an end of season present, and even covered the insurance when 20-year-old James McPike said he couldn't afford it.

Back in 1964, Spanish maestro Alfredo Di Stéfano was taken hostage during Real Madrid's tour of Venezuela. He was eventually let go without any ransom being paid.

Birmingham City were the first club to become a limited company, when, under their original name of Small Heath FC, they incorporated back in 1888.

TOP HEAVY

In 1966, Workington Town in Cumbria expanded their board to 13 members, meaning that they had more directors than players.

Chesterfield were 3–0 up at home to Long Eaton in the Derbyshire Cup in January 2014 when the visitors' keeper got injured. With no replacement on the bench, Chesterfield offered their reserve keeper, Cameron Mason, to the guests. However, the young player didn't manage to keep his own teammates from scoring – conceding four more goals as his temporary side crashed to a 7–0 defeat.

Striker Ian Lawther is the only player to have signed for a Football League club in Parliament. When he moved to Brentford from Scunthorpe United in 1964, the Bees' Chairman was Jack Dunnett MP, who conducted the business inside the House of Commons.

In 2010, Brazilian police stormed the pitch in the game between Genus and Moto Cube when a red-carded player refused his marching orders. The riot gear-clad officers pepper sprayed the guilty party and several other players protesting around him!

An English league match played between Sunderland and Derby County in 1894 will forever be remembered as the 'game of three halves'. With the original referee running late, the game was started with a deputy official, and Sunderland went in 3–0 up at half time. When the original ref arrived at the 45 minute mark, he ordered another full 90 minutes to be played. But the decision didn't help Derby – they shipped a further eight goals over the next hour and a half!

PROST!

Arsenal legend Jens Lehmann was dropped by Stuttgart in 2009 after being spotted at the Munich beer festival without permission. The German goalie had just shipped two goals in a 2–0 defeat to Cologne, and wasted no time in drowning his sorrows just hours after the final whistle.

Argentine midfielder Adrian Bastia received one of the strangest red cards ever, when he tackled a pitch invader in a game between Asteras Tripolis and Panathinaikos in 2008. Sticking out a sneaky leg to trip the intruder, the player was quickly shown a red card for violent conduct, and sent for an early bath.

In 2006, Romanian footballer Marius Cioară was transferred from UT Arad to Regal Hornia for 15 kilograms of sausage meat. He didn't last long – leaving his new club after just 24 hours because of relentless abuse from his teammates when they found out about the, um, tasty transfer fee.

Spanish international keeper Santi Cañizares missed the 2002 World Cup in weird circumstances after dropping a bottle of aftershave on his foot in the team's hotel. A shard of glass penetrated his flesh and he had to be rushed to hospital to undergo surgery.

In 2009, a Spanish referee made history by issuing 19 red cards in one game! As the match between Recreativo Linense and Saladillo de Algeciras descended into a mass brawl, the man in black, Jose Manuel Barro

Escandón, took no prisoners and dished out multiple marching orders.

A KNOCK-OUT PERFORMANCE

When Argentina met the United States in the semi-final of the 1930 World Cup, American physio Jack Coll ran on to the pitch to attend to an injured player. But as he trotted on to the grass, he dropped his medical bag, broke a container of chloroform and the fumes caused him to pass out. In the end it was he, rather than the player, who had to be carried off!

Norman Windram, a lifelong Manchester United fan, watched his first Old Trafford match at four years old, and followed the Reds for over 80 years, attending over 1,800 home matches in a row. It's a record which makes him one of the most loyal supporters in football history.

In 2002, the Chile Under-20 squad were fined by their Football Association for laughing. When someone told a joke which caused the whole team to fall about in hysterics, the coach complained that he couldn't regain authority and control.

CLUCK YOU!

Grimsby Town fan favourite Ivano Bonetti got more than he bargained for in 1996, when his boss Brian Laws is alleged to have thrown a plate of chicken wings at him after the team lost a match. The incident left Bonetti with a fractured cheekbone – and Laws with ten very hungry players.

When Mario Balotelli met a young autograph hunter outside the Manchester City training ground in 2011, he demanded to know why the kid wasn't at school. When the fan explained that he was being bullied, Balotelli promptly went to the school with the boy and his mother, and demanded to see the headmaster to sort the incident out once and for all.

Everton goalie Richard Wright was ruled out of their 2006 FA Cup fourth-round replay at Chelsea after suffering a freak injury during the warm-up. Wright ignored a board warning players not to practice in the goalmouth and promptly fell over the sign, suffering a twisted ankle. The same player also damaged his shoulder falling through a loft as he was trying to pack away his suitcases.

Sheffield United winger Keith Gillespie was sent off just 12 seconds after coming on as a substitute against Reading in January 2007. In fact, it was technically 0 seconds – as the ball hadn't even come back into play when he was dismissed for elbowing Stephen Hunt.

On Christmas Day 1941, Bristol City set off for an away fixture at Southampton. However, with kick-off approaching, only two City players and the team kit had arrived at the Dell – the other two vehicles were nowhere to be seen. Eventually, Southampton helped their guests put together a full team – made up of the two players who'd managed to get there, the Southampton physio, some reserves and three supporters.

THE DOG ATE MY HOMEWORK: FOOTBALL'S FREAKIEST INJURIES

Who and when?	What?	How?
Enner Valencia, West Ham United, 2014–15	Severely cut big toe	Stepped on broken teacup
Dave Beasant, Chelsea, 1993–94	Torn tendon in foot	Tried to control glass bottle of salad cream
Rio Ferdinand, Leeds United, 2001–02	Strained knee ligament	Resting his leg on a coffee table for too long
David Batty, Leeds United, 1990s	Ankle strain	Daughter ran over his foot with tricycle
Alan Wright, Aston Villa, 1990s	Knee sprain	Stretching for accelerator pedal of his new Ferrari
Bryan Robson, England, 1990 World Cup	Broken toe	Lifting and dropping a bed… with Paul Gascoigne inside it
Darius Vassell, Aston Villa, 2002–03	Cut big toe	Tried to pop a blood blister on his toe – with an electric drill
Paulo Diogo, Servette, 2004–05	Lost a finger	Caught his wedding ring on fence whilst running towards fans to celebrate a goal

Who and when?	What?	How?
Adam Chapman, Oxford United, 2012–13	Burnt nipple	Was mixing baby milk topless when disaster struck
Shinji Kagawa, Manchester United, 2013–14	Stomach pumped	The Japan star was taken to hospital after over eating
Liam Lawrence, Stoke City, 2008–09	Twisted ankle	Tripped over his dog and fell down the stairs
Chic Brodie, Brentford, 1969–70	Shattered knee cap	A pitch-invading dog ran into him, causing him to double up in pain
Robbie Keane, Wolves, 1998–99	Ruptured knee cartilage	Stretching to pick up the TV remote
Alex Stepney, Manchester United, 1975	Dislocated jaw	The goalie injured himself barking orders at his defence
Leroy Lita, Reading, 2007–08	Leg muscle damage	Trapped a nerve stretching in bed
Emerson, Brazil, 2002 World Cup	Dislocated shoulder	The defender was playing up to the cameras, saving penalties during a training game

Who and when?	What?	How?
Milan Rapaić, Hajduk Split, 1990s	Eye damage	Stuck his boarding pass into his eye whilst waiting at the airport
Steve Morrow, Arsenal, 1992–93	Broken collarbone	Was dropped after being hoisted by captain Tony Adams after Arsenal won the League Cup in 1993
Diego Maradona, Argentina manager, 2010 World Cup	ten stitches in lip	Got too close to his pet dog, a Chinese Shar Pei, who bit his face
Jari Litmanen, Malmo, 2006–07	Swollen eye	The Malmo Sporting Director, standing next to Jari, opened a can of Coke – and the tab flew into the striker's eye
Charlie George, Arsenal, 1979–80	Lost finger	Had an accident with a lawnmower
Ronaldo, Corinthians, 2009–10	Black eye	The Brazil legend was struck by a microphone in a media scrum as he left the pitch following his debut

COINCIDENCE OR FATE?

Manchester United won the treble (Premier League, FA Cup and UEFA Champions League) in 1999 on what would have been the 90th birthday of their legendary manager Matt Busby (1909–94).

When Fulham midfielder Mousa Dembélé moved across London to Tottenham Hotspur in August 2012, the Cottagers quickly went out to buy a replacement, signing a youngster from Paris Saint-Germain, called – yep – Moussa Dembélé. What a difference an 's' makes.

In 2013–14, Leeds United were managed by Brian McDermott, who had a young winger called Ryan Hall in his squad. At the same time, just 3 miles across the city, Rugby League's Leeds Rhinos' head coach was called Brian McDermott, and they too had a young winger called Ryan Hall in their squad.

WHO'S AFRAID?

Between 1998 and 2003, German club VFL Wolfsburg was managed by the aptly named Wolfgang Wolf.

During the 2012–13 season, Hartlepool United had Peter Hartley and James Poole on their books. In fact, goals from Hartley and Poole gave Hartlepool a 2–1 win over Notts County in February 2013!

Arsenal are sponsored by Emirates Airlines, and as such, their stadium is known as The Emirates. The capital of the United Arab Emirates is Abu Dhabi. In 2006 Arsenal signed midfielder Abou Diaby – and he's still playing in north London to this day.

Manchester United legend Paul Scholes scored on his debut, his 100th game, his 200th game, his 300th game, his 400th game, his 500th game and his 700th game. The only problem? The goal in his 200th outing was in his own net!

On 23 June 2010, half-brothers Jerome and Kevin-Prince Boateng played against each other in the World Cup – the former turning out for Germany, the latter for Ghana.

QPR were in the top-flight relegation zone on the day Margaret Thatcher became Prime Minister, the day she was ousted and the day she died.

In both 2010 and 2012, the following coincidences occurred:

- *Atlético Madrid won the Europa League.*
- *Bayern Munich finished as runners up in the Champions League.*
- *Manchester United finished second in the Premier League, and Spurs finished fourth.*
- *Spain won the major international tournament of that year.*
- *Chelsea won the FA Cup.*
- *Portsmouth were relegated from the Premier League to the Championship.*

The tongue-twisting scoreline, 'East Fife 4 Forfar 5' never actually existed. It was created by comedian Eric Morecambe. However, it nearly became a reality in 2011, when their Scottish Second Division clash finished 'East Fife 4 Forfar 3'.

Defender Dean Richards was involved in three games where his side led 3–0 at half time, only to end up losing – for Southampton against Tranmere Rovers (2001) and for Tottenham Hotspur against Manchester United (2001) and Manchester City (2004).

When Manchester City's Paul Dickov scored an injury-time equaliser at Wembley in the 1998–99 Second Division play-off final against Gillingham, he put the ball past his best man, Gill's keeper Vince Bartram. The goal was voted City's greatest ever in a 2005 poll conducted by the club.

German goalie Hans-Jörg Butt was a skilled penalty taker, scoring three Champions League goals for three different clubs – Hamburg, Bayer Leverkusen and Bayern Munich. The coincidence? They all came against Juventus.

A DIVINE RECORD

Barcelona have played three games during a papal conclave, in 1958, 1978 and 2013, and have won them all 4–0.

David Beckham, who made a career out of whipping in crosses, was born in Whipps Cross Hospital in 1975.

During the 2012 African Cup of Nations, Mali had four midfielders in their squad called Traoré.

In December 2012, UEFA officials got a sense of déjà vu when the official Champions League draw came out exactly the same as the rehearsal draw the day before.

Rumour has it that in 1977, in a game for Carlisle against Crewe at Gresty Road, striker Tommy McElphin hit a thunderbolt of a penalty that hit the crossbar, spooned into the air, flew over the Gresty Road End of the ground and landed on a train that was on the track at the station behind the goal. After the match the Carlisle  team got on the train back to Carlisle, and at the station on their return, McElphin found the very same ball he had struck rolling down the platform.

The 1 July 1976 was an important day for Dutch football – it's the date that Patrick Kluivert and Ruud van Nistelrooy, two of the best Oranje forwards in a generation, were born.

In 2004, Fulham signed Liberian striker Collins John, having had Scottish midfielder John Collins on their books from 2000 to 2003. Collins even introduced John to the confused Craven Cottage crowd upon his signing – because, well, why not?

Since 1970, Italy have made it to the World Cup final every 12 years – in 1982, 1994 and 2006 – lifting the trophy on every second appearance.

Since 2010, Norwich City's first and second choice goalies have been Ruddy and Rudd.

LIKE FATHER, LIKE SON

Cristiano Ronaldo and Lionel Messi were born 869 days apart – exactly the same gap between the birthdays of their respective first-born sons, Cristiano Junior and Thiago.

In 2001, Southampton legend Matt Le Tissier came off the bench to score a last minute winner in the final game ever to be played at The Dell. He said after the game that, on watching his teammates shooting at goal, he hoped it wouldn't go in – so that he would have the honour of being the last scorer at the stadium.

On 11 April 2012, Liverpool's Jon Flanagan lined up in the Premier League against Blackburn Rovers' Bradley Orr – his uncle.

WHERE ARE
THEY NOW?

"

Footballers don't live in the real world… They don't have to grow up. When I retired, I didn't know how to get myself a doctor, or even a dentist.

NEIL 'RAZOR' RUDDOCK

"

Football. It might sound like the dream job, but it's not all money, models and mansions, you know. In reality, for every diamond-encrusted Cristiano Ronaldo, there are jaded journeymen up and down the country with mortgages, school runs and supermarket big shops, just like the rest of us.

So when the years start to tick on, and the legs get heavier, a footballer has to decide what to do when he hangs up his boots. Many make the leap into management, or the media. Some become agents or sports entrepreneurs.

But for others, a life far away from the beautiful game beckons. Doctors, priests, movie stars – they've done it all, from the weird to the wonderful. So next time you meet the milkman on the doorstep, stop and take a closer look. He might just have an international cap or two.

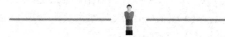

Tony Yeboah

The cult Leeds United hero defined the 1990s long distance wonder goal, leading to thousands of footballs being kicked over garden fences the country over. He also held the record for the only player to have won back-to-back *Match of the Day* Goal of the

Month awards – until Gareth Bale matched him in 2013. But after George Graham took over at Elland Road, Tony was farmed out to Hamburg – and it all went downhill from there. He now runs a chain of hotels in Ghana called Yegoala. Puntastic.

Carlos Roa

The man who broke millions of English hearts when he saved David Batty's penalty to see his Argentina side through to the semi-finals of the 1998 World Cup was subsequently linked with a move to a host of top Premier League clubs – but his career actually took a far more bizarre turn. Just a year after his career peaked on that evening in St Etienne, Roa had devoted himself to religion, gave up meat and moved to a meditation retreat in Mexico. He then returned to the game for a stint at Mallorca – on the understanding that, as a Seventh-Day Adventist, he wouldn't have to play on the Sabbath, which was – you've guessed it – Saturday.

Ken Monkou

After making almost 200 appearances for Chelsea and Southampton during the 1990s, Ken Monkou had a short stint at Huddersfield before retiring to his native Netherlands to open a pancake house in the city of Delft. When he's not tossing, he likes nothing more than to escape to the north of England for a spot of fly-fishing. No, really.

Faustino Asprilla

Newcastle's talented Colombian set the Premier League alight upon his arrival from Parma, even smashing a hat-trick against Barcelona in a 3–2 win for the Toon – but his boss Kenny Dalglish soon ran out of patience with him, and sent him packing back to Serie A. 'Tino', as he is affectionately monikered, attracted controversy at the peak of his career for posing naked on the front of a magazine, and then allegedly firing a shotgun at police (not on the same day). Most recently, he was offered a starring role in a Colombian porn film.

Gabriel Batistuta

Having plundered 168 goals during nine years in Serie A at Fiorentina, 'Bati' moved to Roma and Inter, before making his way to Qatar, the footballing scrapyard, in the early Noughties. So big is his legend in Florence that there is even a statue of the Argentinian striker outside the Stadio Artemio Franchi – and if it ever needs touching up or shifting, perhaps they should call the man himself, as he now owns a construction company back home.

Espen Baardsen

Spurs' old Norwegian stopper, who bagged a Worthington Cup winners' medal in 1999, retired at just 25 years old, claiming that he 'fell out of love with the game' – and went travelling around the world in order to find himself. With himself well and truly located, he has now brought himself back to London, and joined the rat race as a hedge fund manager at an investments firm in the capital.

◇

Bixente Lizarazu

Scrabble top score Bixente Lizarazu spent the 90s flying up and down the left-hand flank for Bayern Munich and his native France, and winning the 1998 World Cup and Euro 2000 (as you do). But age catches up with the best of us, and when his legs started to get a little heavy, he decided to retire from the game to take up less strenuous activities. Like Brazilian jiu-jitsu. He became European Champion after just a year and a half on the mats.

◇

Zvonimir Boban

Croatia's former captain wore the armband at a time when his country boasted a wealth of top talent, including Davor Šuker and Robert Prosinečki. With a reputation for hard tackling and tough battling,

Boban is still a hero in his home country despite kicking a Yugoslavian copper in the face during a pitch invasion whilst he was at Dinamo Zagreb. Following his exit from the pro ranks, Zvonny went from brawn to brains – and completed a university degree focusing on Christianity in the Roman Empire. Today, as well as the odd bit of outspoken punditry work, Boban owns a bar in Zagreb called Boban. Not the most original name, but I'm not going to be the one to tell him, are you?

Neil Webb

The versatile former England star racked up five trophy wins during an illustrious career which saw him turn out for Manchester United, Nottingham Forest, and, erm, Aldershot Town. After hanging up his boots, he went from penalty boxes to post boxes, picking up a mailbag and becoming a postman. He could also occasionally be found flogging programmes outside Reading's Madejski Stadium.

Jorge Campos

He of colourful play and even more colourful jersey was notable for his eccentric style, and, as well as being pretty nifty between the posts, he wasn't half bad up front either – smashing 33 goals in a 16-year career. Turns out, his legendary Mexico goalie top was self-designed (you don't say), but his dodgy fashion sense obviously didn't do him any harm, because he went on to bag 130 caps for his country. He now owns a fast-food franchise back home.

———◇———

Philippe Albert

Perhaps most famous for notching the chipped fifth and final goal in Newcastle's 5–0 demolition of Man United back in 1996, the moustachioed Belgian defender moved to Fulham, before becoming disillusioned with football (well, you can't blame him) and retiring after a short-lived return to Charleroi. His professional career spanned 14 years and 41 international caps, but his life is now more melons than sell-ons, and more citrus zest than fitness tests. Yep, he now works as a greengrocer.

THE QUIZ OF QUIZZES

1) During his time at Liverpool, Uruguayan striker Luis Suárez scored three hat-tricks against the same club. Which club was it?

2) **In 2008, Portsmouth won the FA Cup final. But which team did they beat 1–0 at Wembley?**

3) Which player won 13 Premier League titles, four FA Cups, two Champions Leagues and 64 international caps – but never played at the World Cup finals?

4) **Who finished as top goalscorer in the 2014 World Cup?**

5) Which German legend is credited with inventing the sweeper role?

6) **Which English club has played at Portman Road since 1884?**

7) Which nation played its first official international match on 19 November 2013, battling to a 0–0 stalemate with Slovakia?

8) **Which two cousins lined up for England against Belgium on 10 October 1999?**

9) 'When he told me that he was joining us, the first thing I thought was: "God exists." I think it was the signing of the century!' Which player is Juventus keeper Gianluigi Buffon talking about?

10) **When was Sepp Blatter first elected as FIFA President?**

11) England's 1966 World Cup final win against West Germany is best remembered for Geoff Hurst's hat-trick – but who scored the Three Lions' other goal in the 4–2 victory?

12) **Which nation's top tier is known as the Veikkausliiga?**

13) Who was the only player to notch four goals in a 2014–15 Premier League game?

14) **By what name is Edson Arantes do Nascimento better known?**

15) Which English football club plays at Highbury?

16) **What is so special about the national stadium of Bolivia, the Estadio Hernando Siles?**

17) Who scored the first goal of the 2014 World Cup?

18) **In 2014–15, Sadio Mané smashed the fastest hat-trick in Premier League history at 2 minutes and 56 seconds. Who was he playing for, and which team was he facing?**

19) In 2013–14, Real Madrid's Cristiano Ronaldo smashed a new personal best for goals in one season. How many did he score?

20) **Why does Aldyr Garcia Schlee, an illustrator by trade, hold a surprisingly important place in the history of world football?**

21) When was English League Two side AFC Wimbledon founded?

22) **In 2015, Barcelona won their fifth European Cup – bringing them level with Bayern Munich, and which other club?**

23) West Ham United raised eyebrows when they snapped up two Argentinian internationals in 2006 – who were they?

24) **How much did Real Madrid pay for Colombian superstar James Rodríguez in the summer of 2014?**

25) As of summer 2015, who holds the 15-year-old record for the fastest goal in Premier League history?

26) **In 2015, Swiss club FC Sion won the domestic cup for the thirteenth time in their history – but what's so remarkable about that statistic?**

27) Which nation's domestic league features the teams Hearts of Oak and Heart of Lions?

28) **What was so special about Viv Anderson's 1978 England debut against Czechoslovakia?**

29) Which player did Uruguay striker Luis Suárez bite in the group stage of the 2014 World Cup?

30) **Barcelona defender Gerard Piqué began his career away from Camp Nou – but where?**

QUIZ ANSWERS

Firsts

1) Mexico's Manuel Rosas, versus Chile, 1930.

2) Play at four World Cups without turning out in a single World Cup qualifier.

3) It was the first goal scored in the newly formed Premier League.

4) Iceland's Eidur Gudjohnsen, replacing Arnór Gudjohnsen against Estonia.

5) He became the only player to have scored hat-tricks in the Premier League, Champions League and FA Cup whilst playing for the same club.

6) It made Manchester United the first club to score 1,000 goals in the Premier League.

7) It was the first time that the Premier League introduced a yellow, high visibility ball.

8) He's the first player to score for six different clubs in the competition.

9) Newcastle United's Andy Cole and Blackburn Rovers' Alan Shearer.

10) Peter Schmeichel, playing for Aston Villa in 2001.

11) It was the year that goal nets were introduced for the first time.

12) He was the first manager to be sacked in the Premier League era.

13) He was the first player to score a hat-trick in the Premier League, the Championship, League One, League Two, League Cup, FA Cup and at international level.

14) He smashed a hat-trick as his new club ran out 6–2 victors against Fenerbahçe.

15) The Hatters became the first club in 119 years to go nine games without shipping a single goal.

Managers

1) Roy Hodgson.

2) AFC Bournemouth's Eddie Howe.

3) Republic of Ireland manager Mick McCarthy. The pair had a huge bust up during the 2006 World Cup in Japan and South Korea.

4) 1996.

5) Newcastle United boss Kevin Keegan.

6) Harry Redknapp.

7) Real Madrid's Carlo Ancelotti.

8) Alex Ferguson.

9) Ian Holloway.

10) Brian Clough.

11) They both have the lowest win rates, of any managers who have overseen at least 15 games, in Premier League history – just 18.4 per cent.

12) José Mourinho.

13) He was sent off twice in a game against Coventry City. After the game, he had a strong word with the referee in a managerial capacity, and wound up with a three game touchline ban!

14) Walter Winterbottom.

15) He went to kick the ball back into play and accidentally fouled one of the opposition, sending the bemused player flying down the touchline.

The Men in Black

1) 1970.

2) He became the first referee to officiate the finals of both the UEFA Champions League and the FIFA World Cup in the same year.

3) The kick of death.

4) The referee – the fourth official simply displays the number of minutes.

5) 1996 – Wendy Toms.

6) The Scottish referee dropped his yellow card, and when the playful Geordie handed it back to him, he held it up as if to give a mock booking. Needless to say, Dougie didn't see the funny side.

7) Diego Maradona v England.

8) They were banned from handling the ball outside of their own area.

9) A white handkerchief.

10) He showed Croatia's Josip Šimunić three yellow cards before finally sending the player off in the ninety-third minute.

11) Five feet.

12) According to Law 12, leaving the field of play unless injured without permission is a yellow card offence.

13) No. A referee will always stop the game if he feels an injury is serious, but play can continue until the next stoppage for a minor injury.

14) Nothing, the ball is live. A referee is considered part of the field of play so play goes on as normal.

15) No. The goalkeeper must remain on the line between the posts, facing the penalty taker, until the kick is taken.

16) False. Law 8 states that any player may challenge for the ball, there is no minimum or maximum number.

17) Nothing. The corner flags are considered part of the field of play, so the ball remains live.

18) Law 5 states that if a spectator blows a whistle that the referee believes has interfered with play, he should restart the game with a dropped ball from the position where play stopped.

19) Yes. Law 15 states that goalkeepers are allowed to take throw-ins – although this is rarely seen in practice.

20) A corner kick should be awarded. It's not possible to score an own goal direct from a free kick, so the ball would be treated as if it were out of bounds.

The World Cup

1) Uruguay in 1930. The hosts went on to lift the trophy.

2) He notched his 16th World Cup goal during the tournament in Brazil, the most of any player in history.

3) They have both secured ten clean sheets apiece in the tournament.

4) None.

5) Brazil's Mário Zagallo and Germany's Franz Beckenbauer.

6) Alf Ramsey.

7) Brazil (five).

8) Yugoslavia and Croatia.

9) French striker Just Fontaine scored a whopping 13 goals in one tournament – more than at any other venue in the history of the competition.

10) It was just 11 seconds, and scored by Turkey's Hakan Şükür against South Korea in 2002.

11) West Germany's Helmut Schön, who racked up 25 wins between 1966 and 1978.

12) He is the oldest player to debut at the tournament. He was 39 years, 10 months and 17 days old when he turned out against Algeria in 2010.

13) None.

14) It was his fourth tournament as captain of his national team.

15) He has managed five clubs to the World Cup finals, more than any other coach in history.

The European Championship

1) 1960 in France.

2) Only one – Spain – in 2008 and 2012.

3) The Netherlands' Jetro Willems, at 18 years and 71 days old.

4) It was the first major finals tournament where the players' shirts bore their names as well as their numbers.

5) None.

6) Nine, at France 1984.

7) Henri Delaunay – and the trophy is named after him.

8) They have both appeared at the tournament more than any other player – with 16 appearances apiece.

9) France.

10) Greece – and they lost 1–0.

11) 1972, 1976 and 1980.

12) He's the oldest goalscorer in the tournament's history, at 38 years and 257 days.

13) David Baddiel and Frank Skinner.

14) The Soviet Union and Spain. The Spanish won 2–1.

15) Sixty-eight seconds.

Stadiums

1) It was the first stadium to gain approval to have artificial turf installed.

2) Borussia Dortmund.

3) True.

4) Bradford City's Valley Parade.

5) It's flanked on two sides by the ocean! Bring on the seasickness pills.

6) The Wembley steps. Players trudge up to the royal box to collect their medals after every final.

7) Southend United's.

8) It was Sporting Braga, whose Braga Municipal Stadium is set into the face of a surrounding quarry.

9) A whopping $400 million.

10) Manchester United's Old Trafford.

11) Dundee and Dundee United.

12) Preston North End's Deepdale.

13) The Rungrado May Day Stadium in North Korea.

14) Coventry City's Highfield Road.

15) Manchester City.

Transfers

1) Alan Shearer.

2) Real Madrid.

3) Malmo, Ajax, Juventus, Inter Milan, AC Milan, Barcelona, Paris Saint-Germain.

4) Diego Maradona.

5) He became the first British million-pound player.

6) Italian forward Dani Osvaldo.

7) Preston North End.

8) An extravagant £857 million.

9) He convinced Southampton manager Graeme Souness that he was the cousin of African superstar George Weah.

10) A record-breaking £100.

11) David Luiz.

12) Major League Soccer side New York City Football Club.

13) A set of gym weights.

14) Tottenham Hotspur.

15) His Manchester United teammate Wayne Rooney.

Goalies

1) Lev Yashin of the Soviet Union.

2) The American Samoa keeper shipped 31 goals in a single game against Australia back in 2001 – the most in history.

3) Germany's Jens Lehmann, who ran out against Spain at 38 years and 232 days.

4) The keeper scored over 100 goals in his career, all from free kicks and penalties.

5) He broke his neck during a clash with Birmingham's Peter Murphy – but played on.

6) Spain's Iker Casillas.

7) Shaggy-haired stopper René Higuita, who was playing his club football for Atlético Nacional at the time.

8) He took off his gloves – and went on to score a penalty in sudden death!

9) He scored a hat-trick, dispatching a trio of penalties.

10) He's the only goalie not to have conceded a single goal from open play en route to lifting the trophy.

11) Mexico's Jorge Campos, whose colourful playing attire caught the imagination at the 1994 World Cup in the USA.

12) True.

13) David James, who stopped 13 spot kicks.

14) Italy's Gianluigi Buffon, who switched from Parma to Juventus for a whopping £33 million.

15) He is regarded as the first keeper to use gloves.

Footie Fashion

1) Manchester United and England's Wayne Rooney.

2) In 1907 the club decided to take their colours from the first ship to arrive in the local harbour the next day. It was Swedish, and the rest is history.

3) Notts County.

4) Grey.

5) Kevin Keegan.

6) Arsenal.

7) Cameroon.

8) FC Barcelona.

9) 1939.

10) David Beckham.

11) They began to wear different coloured shirts to the rest of their teammates.

12) St Blaize and Hope Brothers, Bukta, Umbro and Admiral.

13) Apparently he was being paid £52,000 per week at the time.

14) Upon visiting England, the club's captain Perico Escobal noticed the kit worn by Corinthian FC, and rallied for change in order to be more like the English club.

15) Adidas and Puma.

The Quiz of Quizzes

1) Norwich City.

2) Cardiff City.

3) Manchester United and Wales' Ryan Giggs.

4) Colombia's James Rodriguez (six goals).

5) Franz Beckenbauer.

6) Ipswich Town.

7) Gibraltar.

8) Jamie Redknapp and Frank Lampard.

9) Andrea Pirlo.

10) 1998.

11) Geoff's West Ham United teammate Martin Peters.

12) Finland.

13) Manchester City's Sergio Aguero (Manchester City 4–1 Tottenham Hotspur).

14) Pelé.

15) Fleetwood Town in Lancashire. Of course, Arsenal used to play at Highbury in London, before moving to the Emirates Stadium. The old ground was turned into apartments.

16) It's one of the highest stadiums in the world, at 3,637 metres above sea level.

17) Brazil's Marcelo. It was an own goal, but his side eventually beat Croatia 3–1.

18) He was playing for Southampton against Aston Villa.

19) An impressive 61, beating his previous best of 60 (2011–12).

20) At the age of just 18, he won a competition to design Brazil's kit for the 1954 World Cup, changing their white shirts to yellow and green – and the rest is history.

21) 2002.

22) Liverpool.

23) Carlos Tevez and Javier Mascherano.

24) The fee was £71 million, to Ligue 1 side AS Monaco.

QUIZ ANSWERS

25) Ledley King in 10 seconds, Tottenham Hotspur v Bradford City, 9 December 2000.

26) It was only their 13th appearance in the domestic cup final. They've won it every time.

27) Ghana.

28) He became the first black player to play for the Three Lions.

29) Italy's Giorgio Chiellini.

30) Manchester United.

ABOUT THE AUTHOR

Jonno Turner is a writer and social media addict based in Derbyshire. As a football fan chalking up hundreds of miles following his beloved club around the country, he's had plenty of chance to brush up on his knowledge of the game, from the daringly beautiful to the downright bizarre.

Follow Jonno on Twitter:
www.twitter.com/jonnot

THE
FOOTBALL
POCKET
PUZZLE
BOOK

NEIL SOMERVILLE

THE FOOTBALL POCKET PUZZLE BOOK

Neil Somerville

ISBN: 978 1 84953 750 6

Paperback

£5.99

- ⚽ Sudokus
- ⚽ Cryptograms
- ⚽ Crosswords
- ⚽ Acrostics
- ⚽ Picture posers
- ⚽ Word ladders
- ⚽ Word searches

This challenging compendium of brain-teasers about the beautiful game will have you puzzling long after the final whistle has blown.

If you're interested in finding out more about our books, find us on Facebook at **Summersdale Publishers** and follow us on Twitter at **@Summersdale**.

www.summersdale.com